On Our Best Behavior:

Positive Behavior-Management Strategies for the Classroom

Barbara F. Zimmerman, Ph.D.

LRP Publications
Horsham, Pennsylvania 19044

The four-step monitor strategy plan in Chapter 6 written by Meichenbaum and Asarnow was reprinted with permission from Academic Press from *Cognitive-Behavior Intervention: Theory, Research and Procedures,* edited by P.C. Kendall and S.D. Hollon (1979).

Library of Congress Cataloging-in-Publication Data

Zimmerman, Barbara F.
    On our best behavior : positive behavior management strategies for the classroom /
Barbara F. Zimmerman.
        p.   cm.
    Includes bibliographical references.
    ISBN 1-57834-014-4 (alk. paper)
    1. Behavior modification. 2.   Classroom managment. I. Title.

LB1060.2 .Z56 2000
371.102'4--dc21

00-022907

To all the students I have had the privilege of working with and to the children in my life who have never refused to play with me: Mollie, Dana, Rivka, Pini, Adam, Spenser, Laura and Elise

and

In loving memory of Andrea K. Willison, a sensitive and courageous individual

and

Yetta Silverbrand, a woman of wisdom and acceptance

About the Author

Barbara Zimmerman, Ph.D., was a classroom teacher with the Capital Region Board of Cooperative Educational Services in Albany, New York for 12 years. She currently is a Behavior Specialist providing workshops and consultations on positive behavior management for school districts, parents and agencies that work with children and she teaches graduate courses in Emotional Disturbance/Behavior Disorders and Behavior Management at the College of Saint Rose in Albany, New York. Dr. Zimmerman holds degrees in social welfare, educational psychology/special education, and curriculum and instruction from the State University of New York at Albany.

Dr. Zimmerman has worked with behaviorally disordered and emotionally disturbed students, as well as unclassified students, from the pre-school to high school levels. Additionally, she has worked at St. Anne's Institute, a residential facility for emotionally disturbed teen-age girls, and has taught night college courses at New York State Prisons in Wilton and Hudson, New York.

Dr. Zimmerman has had broad experience with disruptive behavior as a former "disrupter," a counselor and a teacher of disruptive students. She has done extensive research on the nature and consequences of classroom disruption and has written a chapter entitled, "Classroom Disruption: Educational Theory as Applied to Perception and Action in Regular and Special Education," in *Advances in Special Education* (JAI Press).

She is a national speaker whose presentations and consultations include positive behavior management techniques for children who exhibit disruptive behavior, as well as general and specific ideas on positive management. Dr. Zimmerman believes children and adults are all individuals who have diverse needs and that optimism, a general concern for people, hard work, clear communication, and a good sense of humor are keys to positive results.

Table of Contents

Preface

This book is designed to provide practical behavior management strategies for educators and parents. It is intended to give suggestions for working and interacting with all children and students, whether they are diagnosed with behavior problems or not. This book provides both theoretical and experiential rationales for the strategies suggested. The strategies are intended to provide home and school environments that foster cooperation and learning. Provided within are specific examples of interventions and strategies that teachers and parents can use immediately. The purpose of including school and home strategies is to promote consistency and cooperation between these two environments in which the child interacts.

For convenience sake, throughout this book, the male gender is used when referring to a person who could be either male or female. No ill intent toward the female gender is implied.

Acknowledgments

I would not have been able to write this book without the assistance and support of many people. I would like to thank Suzanne Bonneville (Chandler), my second-grade teacher, who, in the midst of my academic and behavioral difficulty, told my parents not to worry about me because I had great spirit and would do just fine. She was a wonderful teacher and I have been trying to find her for over a decade to tell her so personally.

Many of my friends and colleagues at the Capital Region Board of Cooperative Educational Services have been important in my development as a Behavior Specialist. I am especially indebted to Wilma, who is the first person I turn to when I don't know something I need to know. And I am indebted to Marie, who is always willing to process with me on a higher level; to Mary, who puts things in proper perspective and makes me laugh, and Colleen, who is fun to joke with about behavior management, political affiliations and the afterlife. I am grateful to Jack, Sandy, Floria, Karen and Jo Anne, who as administrators, always have supported me in my professional pursuits. I am thankful to Candy, who has spent several months of her life on her car phone providing me with important information and emotional support, and Ellen, a great friend and savior who keeps me sane in the office.

I am indebted to my parents, Marvin and Natalie Zimmerman who brought me up in a manner that greatly contributed to my exceeding any expectations I had for myself. I thank my brother Ira who always shared his toys and games with me when we were children. My sister Janie always has been in my corner and as an adult has made me think I can do anything. My stepdaughter and pal, Judith, is a wonderful confidant and buddy with whom I can laugh and cry. Thanks also to Jill, Jackie and Audrey who gave me technical and moral support. And, many thanks to my editor, Maria Neithercott, for her insights and responsiveness.

I have many wonderful friends who are essential to my life. Janet, Joy and Diana have been there for me in the good, the bad and the ugly times.

Lastly and most importantly, I thank Esther Willison whose love and support cannot be measured in words.

Chapter One

Coping, Adapting and Learning: My Personal Experience

I felt inadequate and quite different from everyone else. ...
I masked feelings of inferiority and failure with humor. ...
When I have a goal in mind and enjoy the work, I can
become totally focused and persistent.

On the day that I was born a big ship blew up in the Brooklyn Navy Yard. My mother, in a nearby hospital, heard doctors preparing for a rough night. What a way to come into the world!

I am the youngest of three children; my sister is six years older than I am, my brother is two years older. Both of my siblings excelled in school. My father was a public school teacher who later went on to become a guidance counselor and then an assistant principal. My mother was a housewife who did some secretarial work. We were a typical white middle-class family with the exception of a strong history of bi-polarity (formerly known as manic-depression) on my father's side, and, my history of hyperactivity.

My earliest memories include running — running here, running there, the destination was unimportant, the running was vital. Early recollections are filled with a great deal of frustration. Waiting was impossible. Whatever I wanted, I wanted immediately. I became bored quickly and sought constant activity.

Impulsivity was a consistent theme in my life. I rarely ever thought before I spoke and by the time I thought about the consequences of my actions, the action already had occurred. Among other memories, I remember ruining my brother's beautiful and expensive Lionel train set by impulsively switching a track. The locomotive engine flew off the track, smashed onto the floor and never worked again. I don't remember why I did it, but I do remember feeling dreadful about it, in fact, I still do.

On the outside I had the demeanor of a "happy-go-lucky" kid, but on the inside I was fraught with anxiety and life very often scared me. Little things like learning to tie my shoelaces and to ride a bicycle took me quite a long time to master. My poor father must have taken my training wheels on and off several times. I was unable to do many of the things that my peers could do. Tasks that were easy for them were a mystery to me. One of my friends could spell her entire name, and my name as well, before I could even spell my first name. And, just trying to learn how to tell time was a nightmare.

Although life was difficult in the beginning, it became progressively worse once I started school. Indeed, since almost the first week in kindergarten, I was uncomfortable and unhappy in school. It was impossible for me to stay quiet during naptime, being prone to spontaneous bursts of laughter. I guess I just wasn't tired and sitting for long periods of time was very difficult since I was always in search of adventure. Of course there was that "line thing" too. I couldn't color "within the lines" nor did I enjoy standing "in line" when it was required. And my impulsive behavior also caused many difficult situations.

This pattern continued for much of my elementary years and I progressed to becoming an accomplished "class clown." Teachers reported the same thing from year to year — "Barbara is very immature and quite impulsive." I spent a fair amount of time in the halls, or somewhere else out of the classroom.

It was during second-grade that academic problems surfaced. My handwriting, for example, was absolutely illegible. These problems caused some alarm so I was sent off to the school psychologist who spent a great deal of time administering intelligence tests. During one particular test session the psychologist read a series of numbers which I was supposed to repeat back to him, but instead I found myself absorbed, amazed and fixated on the amount of hair on his hands and never really focused on the numbers. Once again the report read, "Barbara is very immature and impulsive."

I also had a great deal of difficulty with math. I was able to memorize math facts quickly but had a terrible time doing computation, mostly because I never could line up the numbers appropriately. I made careless mistakes all the time and couldn't seem to complete assignments. I avoided doing schoolwork and homework because the results only reinforced my feelings of inadequacy. My papers came back looking bloodstained due to all the red correction marks. (Later on when I became a teacher I refused to use a red pen to make corrections on a student's work. I used green.) Often I had to re-do entire assignments because they were either unreadable or incomplete. At times I had to do assignments several times over. The quality never improved and usually the teacher would give up and accept the work as it was, shaking his head at me disapprovingly. I always did just enough to get by and most of the time I did. I was told to "try harder, apply yourself, and stop being lazy".

I did have some teachers who were nurturing and structured — two very important elements for me. Under their direction I responded positively and excelled. My second-grade teacher handled my hyperactivity and inability to complete assignments with a firm but gentle hand and I have fond memories of her. I also remember my ninth-grade math teacher who spent her after-school hours guiding me and helping me prepare for the Algebra Regents exam. Even though my guidance counselor had written me off as an irresponsible and an unmotivated student who also had a "math block," I earned a 92 on the Regents.

Unfortunately, I have many more memories of teachers who were rigid, unimaginative and used heavy doses of humiliation to get me to do the things they thought I should be able to do. My fourth-grade teacher sent me to the kindergarten room because "I was a baby." A particularly nasty memory is of my sixth-grade teacher calling me to the front of the room and slamming me in the back of the head with a math book with enough force to send my glasses flying across the room. My offense was twofold: I didn't know the answer to the problem on the board, and I didn't have my math book open to the correct page.

As I grew older my sense of self-worth was quite poor. I was particularly sensitive and my feelings often were hurt. I was particularly susceptible to teasing, which made me a prime target for it. I felt inadequate and quite different from everyone else. I had few friends at the beginning of my life, and the friends I chose either led me into mischief, abused me in some way, or had worse social skills than I did. I masked feelings of inferiority and failure with humor and my sole intent in life was to make others laugh *with* me, hoping, though, that they wouldn't laugh *at* me.

Things started to look up in high school. My involvement in a variety of activities helped. I played in the band, sang in the choir, worked in the library and was the first girl in my high school to letter in four sports. This type of schedule worked well for me. It satisfied my energy needs, provided me with variety and offered me the chance to meet students who were positive role models, some of whom became my friends and all of whom were motivated to get good grades. This was inspirational for me and in the subjects I liked, history and English, I did quite well. Math and science, however, always remained a problem. My class schedule was quite bizarre. I was in the high-track social studies class, the middle track for most of the others, but in math and science I was in the lowest group made up of "the expendable students," the ones who were headed for a dead-end life. School was a confusing and sometimes painful experience but I managed and, although not a great student, I had enough savvy to make my way through the system.

My parents wanted me to become a schoolteacher or a librarian. Although I come from a long line of teachers, but am somewhat rebellious, I decided not to follow the pattern. Being a librarian was totally out of the question for me, since librarians are supposed to maintain order not encour-

3

age chaos. I was accepted into a competitive university because I was an excellent tennis player and consequently made the varsity tennis team as a freshman. But I became quite anxious when the time came to leave for college and I started to have second thoughts about going at all. My parents insisted that I go so I decided to talk to my guidance counselor about my anxieties. His words of comfort to me were, "Don't worry, Barbara, if you study really hard and work really hard you'll probably get Ds and maybe some Cs." I ended up leaving for college with a deep sense of fright.

But once there I threw myself into a frenzy of activity. I played on the tennis team, worked in the cafeteria and later became a residence assistant. The busier my schedule, the more comfortable I felt — a pattern that would repeat itself throughout my life. However, I was having huge adjustment problems. I drove my roommate crazy with my constant flurry of movement. Fortunately she was firm with me yet kind in her delivery of the message. We remain good friends today and often laugh about those "crazy" days.

In spite of my forgiving roommate it was still a very difficult time. I became more acutely aware of being different and after the fall tennis season was over I fell into a deep depression. I began to develop intense stomach problems associated with the difficulties I was experiencing. During a school break, my mother took me to a doctor who diagnosed me as being hyperkinetic. Back in 1974 very little was known, or at least I didn't know anyone who knew much, about this hyperkinetic thing (later to be called hyperactivity and still later to be called Attention Deficit Disorder). The medical advice the doctor gave me seems laughable now. He told me to slow down and relax or else I would get an ulcer. Unfortunately either he was not able to, or at least didn't tell me how to do either. (Later on, as an adult, I was diagnosed with Attention Deficit Hyperactivity Disorder and left the doctor's office with a prescription for Ritalin. I don't use Ritalin regularly, but on an "as-needed" basis and it has been extremely helpful.)

Eventually my roommate encouraged and convinced me to go to the university's counseling center. The therapist was excellent and helped me with many of my issues. Most importantly, she taught me how to separate my feelings one by one and deal with them individually instead of having them lumped together in one giant jumble of distress. She taught me how to begin using organizational tools such as making schedules and prioritizing. She taught me how to listen to my body and suggested that when it required movement to move. I began to be able to predict what would be a difficult situation and I learned how to strategize to make it easier. This organization thing was incredibly amazing to me and I began to do what many females with Attention Deficit Disorder do — I started to overcompensate. I realized that since I had such little internal control the best way for me to survive was to develop as much external control as possible. It's what I now have come to call "external scaffolding" — the development of an organizational system to help make order out of chaos. I began to insist on order in my surroundings. It was in college that I started to become obsessed with arranging and rearranging things to make them more organized. I all but eliminated the problem of procrastination by doing a task as soon as I got it. Putting off something made me feel anxious and then I would start to feel overwhelmed.

I decided to become a social worker in my second year at college and, for perhaps the first time in my life, not only did I enjoy schoolwork, but I also excelled at it. I graduated with honors and two weeks later found myself working as a counselor at a residential facility for teen-age girls. These girls, for the most part, who had many problems in their schools and communities, were sent to the facility by the courts of New York State. Most of the girls were not much younger than I was at the time, and I learned a great deal from them for which I am very thankful. It was a very difficult job as the facility often was understaffed and the burnout rate was quite high. However, it was a rite of passage for me and the experience helped shape my future endeavors. I worked there for two years, but after I was rendered unconscious in an altercation, I decided to go back to school.

With my newfound adult perspective on life, I decided to stop being rebellious and become a teacher as I always really had wanted to do, but was too stubborn to admit. I received my master's degree in Educational Psychology/Special Education and was lucky to secure a job immediately after I graduated. My teaching career includes one year in high school, three years in elementary and the last eight years I spent teaching in a middle school. The majority of students with whom I worked were labeled emotionally disturbed; many of them had Attention Deficit Disorder and/or had a learning disorder. Teaching suited me well. Every day was a different experience. I tried to do a lot of hands-on activities and alternated sedentary tasks with more lively activities. I scheduled the days into 20 to 30 minute segments. This type of schedule not only benefited the students but also was perfect for me.

Some of the students had incredibly difficult lives. Many were inner-city kids with abusive parents, minimal supervision and problems far worse than mine. It was very difficult to deal with the problems these students faced or the problem of how to find solutions to make it better.

These students were a reflection of society's failures. They entered the school system with a tremendous amount of "baggage." Some came very badly damaged, while others weren't too bad off but became worse once they were well integrated within the system. They did not trust anyone and I couldn't think of too many reasons why they should. For the most part these students were treated as pariahs and were confronted with prejudices that elicited comments such as some I often overheard in the faculty room — "He can't help it, he's emotionally disturbed." "He's so hyper. Just look at his home life."

Basically those kids didn't care about the state education mandated curriculum, and, for the most part, they didn't care about passing any New York State competency exam. But, they did want to learn. They wanted to learn much more than anyone could imagine.

After my own school experience and 12 years of teaching, I've come to realize several things. If a student does not feel safe physically and emotionally, that student will not learn. If a student does not feel respected by the person trying to teach him, that student will not learn. If the curriculum is not relevant and interesting to the student, that student will not learn. The students with whom I worked were a difficult, yet exhilarating crew. There were days when I came home exhausted and miserable, yet there were days when I came home energized and ecstatic. Some students may never learn all that they should, but they always will learn something. It seems to me that when students feel secure, comfortable, welcomed and happy, they will learn. They will learn even if you do not try to teach them anything.

Whenever it was possible, and as often as I could, I left it up to my students to decide what I should teach. I guess I was more fortunate than most teachers were in having this luxury. To be honest, if my students didn't kill each other or destroy valuable property during the school year, then the administration considered the year to be a success. If, also, by chance the students happened to learn something it was considered to be "gravy."

My classroom was self-contained. It was a rare occurrence when an administrator came in. Naturally, this left me with a tremendous amount of power which I was quite willing to share with my students, benefiting them as well as myself. The students were given a voice as I tried to make sure that they were heard. Their desires and expectations were respected, although not always met. Hopefully, they gained some self-confidence and learned how to make choices that would prove to be successful and gratifying. As for myself, I've learned an amazing amount of information during my 12 years of teaching.

Of course, I was not totally autonomous. There were some curricular requirements to which I had to adhere. There also were subjects and topics that I felt were very important for my students to learn. Sex and drug education are two examples that come to mind. There were times when I had to do a good "soft-shoe" act to motivate my students to participate in some curriculum that I felt was important, but one that they didn't find amusing. However, because they most often had a choice, they usually trusted me and followed my lead. The classroom did not always run smoothly, but, then again, I never expected it to. In fact, very often it was during the times when it was not running smoothly, that we all learned the most.

Many of the students who walked through the door of my classroom had tremendous emotional issues with which to deal and most could not even identify what they were feeling. This combination very often led to some disturbing, even dangerous, disruptions. In my 12 years of teaching I saw books, pencils and furniture fly. I dealt with students who would totally shut down and would not attempt to start an assignment, much less complete it. I heard students verbally berate each other with such ferocious force that I would feel like crying and I had students who would question, challenge and fight me on every decision that I made. As I previously mentioned, I tried to give my students choices and I tried to communicate a feeling that I would like them no matter what they did. I also let them win some of the battles and I tried to empower them by sharing my power. Very often, however, it just was not enough.

In order to provide what I thought was an environment conducive for learning and creating positive social interactions, I used two behaviorist techniques — behavior charts and contracts. All of my students were given individualized behavior charts, and each student would decide on which behaviors they would focus. The students would work for checkmarks and for small daily rewards and a larger weekly reward. Additionally, every year at least one to three students were on a behavior contract that was tailor-made for each student. When a student was having particular problems and seemed receptive to using a contract, we would negotiate together in terms of the things I wanted and the things that the student wanted.

Employing techniques from the humanistic theory, I conducted class meetings where students would have an opportunity to voice their opinions. Using principles from the cognitive theory, I tried to teach my students to "think about their thinking." I used this technique to assist them with issues of anger and impulsiveness. These methods worked quite well for most of my students, but particularly well for the students who had behavior problems.

I felt successful as a teacher, although I'm sure there are those who have had greater success. I always was comfortable with my eclectic style, although, admittedly I did not think much about theory. In the actual running of a classroom, I think teachers do what they can to have successful programs and don't really concentrate or think too much about what theory they're operating under. How they choose to structure their classrooms depends on many things, including their own school experiences, the training they have, their teaching experience and the students with whom they work.

To supplement my workday I scheduled many activities after school. Sporting events were important to me. I participated in tennis, bowling and speed walking. I stripped and refinished the woodwork in my entire house, built a large deck with my partner and coached a boys' high school varsity tennis team. I also had a night job. I taught remedial math at a local medium security prison to inmates who were working toward earning an associate's degree. This was quite an interesting and satisfying experience for me. Friends would tease me, insisting that I probably was just "doing time there."

Unfortunately in my late-20s and early-30s I began to have medical problems that were taking a toll on my body. I was diagnosed with Sclero-derma, a rheumatological autoimmune disease. My joints ache regularly and I am prone to infections caused by an overproduction of calcium in my system. Some of these infections land me in the hospital—a horrible place for anyone, particularly someone with Attention Deficit Disorder. Sadly, one by one, I was forced to drop different sports activities from my life. This was a major blow to me since sports activities were a way to satisfy my need for activity, variety and success, and in the worst times of my life this was one area that gave me a feeling of positive self-worth. As my activity level became more limited I became more and more miserable and difficult to be around. I would snap angrily at people and seemed to lose my sense of humor. A friend suggested I go back to school and work on earning a doctorate. My immediate reaction was "no way," but the next day I went to the local university and made plans to apply to the Curriculum and Instruction Program. I completed my doctorate program in only four-and a-half years and it took me less than a year to complete my dissertation. I enjoyed doing research and studied my favorite topic. My dissertation is titled "The Nature and Consequences of Classroom Disruption." When I have a goal in mind and enjoy the work I can become totally focused and persistent.

I am no longer working in the classroom. For the past seven years I have been a consultant, working with teachers, psychologists, administrators and other educational staff providing workshops and individual consultations for students who exhibit disruptive and dangerous behavior in school. Additionally, I work with parents on similar issues. I hold workshops and training sessions and work with educational personnel and parents on developing positive and humane behavior intervention plans. This is another job that suits me well. It offers variety and I get to travel and spend most of my days speaking and working with people on a subject about which I feel passionate. It is ironic that I spent my childhood with people telling me to, "Sit down and be quiet," and now people ask me to "stand up and talk."

I still have Attention Deficit Disorder. I did not "grow out of it." I'm able to cope with it better than I used to, but I have to monitor myself constantly. I still have trouble knowing where I am in space and time and therefore I have to surround myself with clocks, watches and calendars. I can perseverate on ideas or events that have occurred years ago or on events that will not happen for months or even years to come. Changes in routine make me nervous and anxious but I have learned to plan for them and anticipate strategies. I often visualize and imagine myself in situations that are difficult and play them out in my head. I still am quick to overreact. I can get angry in a split second, for example when I can't find something I'm looking for, when plans change unexpectedly or when I'm trying to assemble something. I still have a tendency to answer a question before the person asking is finished speaking and I have to work very hard on not interrupting people. I have difficulty being "in the moment." While I'm in the middle of one project, I'm thinking about the next one. As I did when I was a child, I'm usually still chewing the last bite of my meal while I'm washing the dishes. I can now recognize when these things occur and have learned to take deep breaths, count in my head, and, when necessary and possible, to take a walk and remove myself from the situation. I still crave variety and like new and different things. It's almost embarrassing to admit that I have owned nine cars in 13 years. Usually these cars are bought when I'm in an impulse mode. The last car was bought on a day when I woke up and said, as I left the house in the morning, "I'm going out to look at some cars." I didn't even know which car I wanted, but by the afternoon I not only had bought a new car, I drove it home. After the impulsive moments I fret for days about whether I did the right thing, talking on and on about it, driving my partner crazy.

Sitting continues to be a problem, so I get up and move around during those times when I have a significant amount of work to do at my desk. I seek out people to chat with and I leave little "mindless" tasks around to do and toys to play with when I take a break. I am driven to having a project or to do something that I think is "useful." I live by writing lists. I've been known to write a list of my lists. I am obsessively organized, everything needs to be color-coordinated and I spend many hours reorganizing my workspace. I am a slave to this compulsion but it gives me comfort and I couldn't function without it. There are thoughts written down on pieces of paper and lists all over my house, my car and my office.

Making people laugh continues to be one of the greatest pleasures I have. However, I've become much better at filtering my remarks, knowing that not everything I think is funny is funny to everyone else. I have fond memories of cracking up a whole class of serious doctoral students, including the professor, when I was working on my degree. I also have a very tolerant boss who usually laughs at all my jokes even when I spit out one-liners like machine-gun fire during staff meetings. I have had a room of 200 professional educators hysterical during workshops that I give and it makes me feel great! I am still in constant search of new activities and I'm still always on the run. Not surprisingly, my favorite T-shirt says, "Blowing the lid off boredom." I still make questionable judgments like owning and riding a motorcycle for several years without having a license. It reminded me of the thrill I got as a kid of riding my bicycle without brakes. It was always an adventure. Additionally, my partner complains that I quickly lose interest in things and I usually have to be corralled to just sit and talk. Perhaps, the biggest demon I battle on a daily basis is the feeling that one day I will wake up and everyone will have figured out that I am an impostor. As successful as I have fortunately become, I constantly fight that nagging voice in the back of my head that says, "You're stupid"!

I know that I am one of the lucky ones. Many more people with Attention Deficit Disorder are not as lucky as I. I was able to gain some self-insight, learn how to monitor my behavior and sometimes have my ADD work as an advantage for me. Many people suffer horribly both in childhood and adulthood, being unable to hold onto jobs or stay in a committed intimate relationship. There are several reasons why I believe my story has a happy ending. One of the biggest reasons is that I do not have any other type of processing problem besides my ADD. There are people who have disabilities in conjunction with their Attention Deficit Disorder, such as Tourettes syndrome or a severe learning disability. I had the academic ability needed and when I was able to use it, I was usually successful.

I also have to credit my parents who believed in a great deal of structure. Bedtimes were set and I always knew what was going to happen if I behaved in a certain manner. Somewhat unusual is the fact that I behaved better at home than at school. Limits were clearly set at home and, although as a child I bucked and fought against the structure, when I grew into adulthood I realized that this structure was my salvation.

Additionally, I was extremely fortunate throughout my life to have some very supportive and understanding friends. I met one of my closest friends in Hebrew School. She was, and still is, a loyal friend who looks up to me. Before that time I didn't believe anyone could look up to me. She helped me gain a tremendous amount of confidence and she was an excellent role model. Even at the tender age of 10 she had a good handle on what was really of value in life. She still is a close friend and, consistent with her supportive nature, revels in my success.

I mentioned previously my college roommate, who also remains a friend today. She was there at a critical time when I was coming to realize that my life had to change. Again, she was an excellent role model and although I annoyed her with my behavior, she was always there for me. I met another one of my wonderful friends while I was interning as a social worker. She was assigned as my field work supervisor. Later on we became good friends, although our relationship at the beginning was more of therapist/patient. I believe I owe her thousands of dollars in therapy costs! She is the type of person who usually knows what's going on with me before I do and it was she who suggested I go back to school. As impulsive and horrible as some of my choices have been, I was lucky to have made some truly excellent choices of friends. I believe strongly that I would not be the person I am today without them.

Although I did suffer from a very poor self-image I had two things going for me that continually helped build my confidence. One was my athletic ability that earned me accolades and praise. The other factor was my ability to make people laugh. Although it often got me in trouble in school, when I left a classroom of laughing students to go to the detention room, I knew I had scored with my classmates.

Most importantly, I've been very lucky to have lived with a partner for the last 18 years who has been a rock throughout the trials and tribulations of my life. My partner understands me like no other and often helps to ground me, constantly reminding me and helping me to stay in the moment. A supportive statement such as, "I don't want to fight so I am reminding you we have to leave in 45 minutes" helps me to get my act together to make sure I am on time. Controversy is avoided with a pre-set such as, "Don't get angry but..." Perhaps most importantly, my partner makes me believe that I can do anything I set out to do. Whether you have Attention Deficit Disorder or not, everyone should have a partner like mine.

Life can be a struggle at times, but I know that I can win most of the battles most of the time. I often think about how lucky I am!

Chapter Two

Introduction

Even when we have an operational definition of "inappropriate behavior" there are so many different opinions about how to deal with that behavior. ... Perhaps the first place to look when dealing with the inappropriate behavior of others is within ourselves.

As a former classroom disrupter and teacher of students with behavior problems, behavior management always has been a topic of interest to me. Although, discussing the topic can be tricky business. The concept of behavior management can raise issues that may ignite emotion. A child's inappropriate behavior can send the most competent and confident adult into a furious spasm of self-doubt.

One of the reasons behavior management is so tricky or complex is that the perception of what is or is not "inappropriate behavior" is in the "eye of the beholder." What one person finds charming and delightful behavior, others may find rude and inappropriate. Even when we have an operational definition of "inappropriate behavior" there are so many different opinions about how to deal with it. Dealing with the behavior of others is based on many factors, such as the personality traits of those involved, how the person who is doing the discipline was disciplined as a child, the environment in which the behavior and discipline occur, and the state of mind of the child and the adult.

Additionally, when we think of behavior management we have to remember behavior is dynamic. It lives, breathes and changes according to the circumstances in which it occurs. As is often the case in some situations — when you fix something, something else breaks — so it can be when dealing with behavior.

Being a parent or teacher of a child who exhibits problematic behavior has always been a difficult task, and some individuals may feel that the job gets tougher and tougher. It helps to remember that children who display difficult behavior don't stay up all night thinking of ways to torture the adults in their lives, even though, at times, it is tempting to think so. Disruptive children want what most children want — to be accepted, loved and validated — but something in the disruptive child's life short-circuits this goal.

Perhaps the first place to look when dealing with the inappropriate behavior of others is within ourselves. Parents and teachers should examine their own perceptions of what inappropriate behavior is and how it should be dealt with, especially when dealing with disruptive children. In short, examine your own baggage. If an adult can't control his own behavior, he certainly will not be able to help a child control his behavior.

Certainly, behavior management is a complicated phenomenon. Even in the best of circumstances, with the best intentions, things can go horribly wrong. My mother always says, "Mensh tract und Gut lacht," which roughly translated means, "A person plans and God laughs." Try not to be too hard on yourself when dealing with behavior. If you are having a difficult time remember you are not alone. People before you have struggled and people will struggle after you. I hope this book provides some insight and assistance in dealing with difficult behavior.

The Problem of Inappropriate Disruption

Disruptive actions of both a minor or more serious nature are commonly experienced by teachers and can present an interruption to normal teaching and learning (Clarke, Parry-Jones, Gay and Smith 1981). Classroom disruption is becoming a grave matter as antisocial and aggressive behavior escalates in the schools. This kind of disruption is a major source of concern for school officials and society at large (Walker and Sylvester 1991) since the single best predictor of adolescent criminal behavior is a long-established pattern of early school antisocial behavior (Patterson and Bank 1986).

One of the primary goals of education is to provide an appropriate atmosphere in which to teach academic skills, while another important goal is to instill values that are consistent with successful functioning in society. It is believed that both the individual and society will be served by fulfilling these goals. Dealing with the disruptive actions of students will have an impact on the actions that these students will choose in their future lives; actions that may, in turn, impact their communities and society as a whole (Zimmerman 1998).

Because the process of teaching often is interrupted by what are conceived to be disruptions, teachers and other educational staff find themselves in the role of disciplinarians. They face the daily challenge of implementing educational strategies suitable for increasing student motivation to participate, and for encouraging non-disruptive actions from those students. The degree to which classroom teachers are meeting this challenge has been the subject of many public debates. Professional educators agree that poorly selected and implemented disciplinary techniques have a negative influence on students and teachers. The effect on students of these inadequate disciplinary techniques is documented by the fact that discipline problems are the major cause of student referrals made by regular educators to special education and the influence of discipline-related problems on teachers has been identified as the prime stress-producing factor in teaching (Smith and Misra 1992).

Also, with the current trend of integrating and including students with disabilities into regular education programs, the issue of disruption in the classroom becomes even more important (Zimmerman 1995). The benefits of inclusion have been documented revealing the positive effect inclusion can have on everyone in a classroom. "Disabled students become more confident and independent, and their classmates learn tolerance" (Parsavand 1994, p. A1). However, inclusion does bring up new concerns and issues.

Many teachers in inclusionary situations often feel overwhelmed by having to work with too many students with special needs. "For many of these teachers, accommodating the students' academic and behavioral difficulties requires considerable effort or may even necessitate instructional expertise they have not yet acquired" (Heckman and Rike 1994, p.30). The American Federation of Teachers has stated publicly their opposition to "full inclusion," pointing out that teachers are not adequately trained to deal with the wide range of disabilities, physical and emotional (Feldman 1994). It should be noted, however, that in any event, issues of disruption, whether caused by the classroom environment or caused by individual students, need to be addressed. It is the opinion of this writer that the time has come to start training all teachers (special and regular educators) in the same manner.

An important factor to consider when thinking about classroom disruption is individual students and teachers, as well as other staff members may have different interpretations of what constitutes a disruptive action. Another point to keep in mind is that not every disruptive action is unwarranted. In some cases, the disruptive actions of one student may be essential for his emotional or physical welfare. Even with this in mind, however, one of the most serious issues facing teachers is the presence of challenging behaviors such as aggression, swearing, defiance or other disruptive acts (Foster-Johnson and Dunlap 1993). It is important to gain an improved understanding of the disruptive actions of students and to deal effectively with such disruption.

Understanding the home environment of disruptive students is equally important. When students come from what is typically thought of as a dysfunctional home, the likelihood of disruptive behavior increases. Although

15

one should not assume children coming from stable and caring homes never exhibit inappropriate behavior in school. The disruptive actions of a child in the home environment can have a serious impact on the entire family and home life. Minor disruption is expected from all family members; however, when disruptions escalate to the point of constant out-of-control behavior, intervention is essential. When dealing with disruptive behavior at home, or in the school, a consistent approach, one that makes sense to the child, should be employed. For that reason, both school and home strategies will be discussed in this book. One of the intentions of this book is to provide educators with information and tools to assist parents in recognizing and dealing with inappropriate behavior. When inappropriate behavior is decreased at home there is usually a noticeable improvement in the school environment.

Chapter Three

General Guidelines for Positive Behavior

When dealing with a specific behavior it is important to find the cause in order to understand why it is occurring. Quite often inappropriate actions are displayed as a device to communicate a need or a want.

I always stress the need for creating an environment that is conducive for cooperation and positive social interaction. In general it is best to "choose your battles." Try and ignore as much inappropriate behavior as possible. Give children choices for behavior whenever possible, keeping in mind inappropriate behavior should not be inadvertently rewarded. Often children use inappropriate behavior to avoid situations that are unpleasant to them. If you notice an escalation in inappropriate behavior 10 minutes before math class and the result of this escalation is removal of the student from the class, you may be "feeding into" exactly what the student wants — to avoid math. The same would hold true at home. If a child does not like doing the dishes and breaks a dish every time this chore is assigned, a parent eventually may get fed up and not allow the child to do the dishes anymore. The consequence then is a reward for inappropriate behavior. If this occurs regularly, a different strategy would be advised.

Another thing to be careful about is not verbally beating up on a child when they do a "good" job. For instance, avoid saying things like, "Oh, so you can do that" or "Why can't you do that everyday"? There will be days when a child will perform well and days when he will not. This is something that he may not be able to control.

Additionally, I have heard adults say, "She did that on purpose," or "He planned it out"! Children, at times, do plan things out, but children with chronic behavior problems generally do not. They don't think things out to final conclusions or think about the consequences of actions, which may lead to some horrendous judgment calls.

There is no single or best method for dealing with children with behavior difficulties and it sometimes can be a frustrating experience for all concerned. Try to stay calm, because the child relies on the teacher, the parent and other adults to be in control.

17

When dealing with a specific behavior it is important to find the cause in order to understand why it is occurring. Quite often inappropriate actions are displayed as a device to communicate a need or a want. (Further discussion of this issue will follow in Chapter Five.) Below are 10 tips for creating a positive environment in which a child will function more aptly. It is important to follow these tips at home as well as in the classroom in order to ensure a positive environment.

10 Tips for a Positive Environment

1. *You must respect the child.*

a. Children learn how to respect others when they are respected themselves.

2. *Set consistent rules and limits.*

a. The child must be clear on "how far" he can go. If there is no limit the child will have no idea when to stop. This can cause some significant disruptive behavior.

b. Children can become extremely anxious without limits. It is a comfort to the child to know someone is in charge who will not let things get too out of control.

c. Rules should be clear and direct. The child should understand what they are supposed to do.

d. Rules should be reasonable and achievable. Try not to set up the child for failure by asking him to do things of which he may not be capable. (For example, being assigned schoolwork that is too difficult without appropriate teacher assistance or being made to sit in Aunt Bertha's living room for more than a half-hour with nothing to do while the adults talk.)

e. There must be follow-through on consequences. If the rules are broken be sure to follow-through with an appropriate consequence or these rules will be broken again. This is also true for rewarding appropriate behavior. If an agreement is made between a child and a teacher/parent for a reward for certain behavior the reward must be given if the child lives up to his end of the bargain. When follow-through is non-existent, or inconsistent, children learn not to trust the adult, or worse, they learn not to take the adult seriously. It's better to have no rules at all than to have rules with no follow-through.

3. *Use positive reinforcement.*

a. Reinforce appropriate behavior. Instead of the "squeaky wheel getting the grease," reward children who demonstrate appropriate behavior.

b. The rule for positive reinforcement is to deliver it often. This is particularly true for children who tend to suffer from low self-esteem. They need to hear praise frequently.

c. Keep in mind that individual children may need different amounts.

d. The praise you deliver should be specific, honest and sincere. Children become resentful when they feel an adult is complimenting them to manipulate them.

4. *Include children in decisions about behavior and discipline.*

a. Imposing all the rules yourself is not a good idea. By including the child you make him feel as if he is part of the plan. You are doing it with him, not to him.

b. Give the child choices for behavior whenever possible.

c. When a child is displaying inappropriate behavior ask him for his suggestion on what may be a more appropriate way to act.

d. Rules generated by children are adhered to more diligently.

e. Including children in issues of behavior helps them to mature. They will look more closely at their needs and monitor their own behavior.

5. *Be yourself with children. Share yourself with them.*

a. Children care about you and want to know who you are. Give them opportunities to show their sensitivity to you.

b. Be open, honest and direct.

6. *Be available emotionally and physically.*

7. *Avoid power struggles — push and pull situations.*

a. "Choose your battles."

b. Demonstrate compromise.

8. *Every action causes a reaction. Children should understand that there are always consequences for behavior. There are two types of consequences:*

a. "Imposed consequences" are consequences that would not necessarily follow in the natural environment. Assigning a student detention for not doing homework or grounding a child for coming home late are two examples.

b. "Natural consequences" are a direct result of actions that occur within the environment. For example: When a child acts in an inappropriate manner other students may laugh at him. Or, when a child throws a favorite toy on the floor in anger and it breaks that child loses the opportunity to play with the toy. Natural consequences are more meaningful to individuals therefore they have the greater strength in effecting a behavior change.

9. *Be good role models for children. They will follow your lead!*

10. *Laugh as much and as often as possible. You really cannot work and be with children unless you can appreciate the joy and humor that this responsibility brings.*

Chapter Four

School Environment

So often it is the student with behavior problems who is the target of extra help. ... Letting these students know that you feel they have something to give is a terrific confidence booster.

Structure and Consistency

Structure and consistency are important for all students, but vital for students with chronic behavior difficulties. As previously mentioned, students need to know just how far they can go, and when they do go too far they need to see consequences for their actions. On some level it is a tightrope act. As a teacher, you may question whether you're being too rigid or too lenient, but you'll get clues to the answers to these questions by the response you get from the student. It can be frustrating because the student with behavior problems tends to resist structure or what he may see as constraints. Yet, without this structure a student can become lost, frustrated and even hostile.

Consistency is as important as structure in working with the student with behavior problems because these students rely on consistency and set patterns established in the classroom. Consistency also is critical since students with behavior problems usually are not able to predict their environment as successfully as other students. They are not good observers of others' behavior (or their own), nor do they have a good sense of time. As a result, they have difficulty predicting what will happen unless a consistent and well-publicized plan is in place. Changes in routine and changes in the way behavior is handled can send that student into a tailspin.

Follow-through is essential to maintaining structure and consistency. The student with behavior problems must see consequences for both appropriate and inappropriate behavior and these consequences should be delivered in a calm and swift manner.

Providing a "stress-free zone" in the classroom adds to the student's structured surroundings and is a way of creating a space where, either by the student's choice or the teacher's choice, an agitated or disruptive student can get his act together. You can set up a stress-free zone taking into consideration your own needs and style as well as the needs and style of the students. Some examples I've seen are study carrels, bean bag chairs, regular chairs and rug areas. I know one teacher who even built a cardboard space ship in her classroom. It is important to remember that these areas should not be used as punishment, but rather as therapeutic tools to assist a student who is temporarily disruptive. It is a space where he can collect himself and prepare to return to the group. It also can be used for students who recognize they are having difficulty and request private space. The area should be inside the classroom so the student is still hearing and seeing what's going on in the classroom, which may motivate him to rejoin the group.

Building Self-Esteem

Increasing a student's self-esteem also may curtail disruptive behavior. Students with behavior problems seem particularly vulnerable to having low self-esteem. As these children get older and start to feel different from others, they tend to compare themselves with their peers, unfavorably, and feel badly about themselves. Adding to their predicament they also must endure the ridicule of other students as well as adults. The best way to combat this is to start to build their confidence before these negative feelings begin. Below are some strategies on how to do this:

Assign responsibilities: There are a million chores to be done in a classroom and I believe all students should have a part in doing them. For the student with behavior problems, chores are wonderful. They provide a variety of activities and help make the student feel capable. All of my students had weekly jobs, but I made sure there were extra jobs for those students who wanted and needed them. I always had three or four staplers in my room, as stapling papers was a favorite activity for many of my students. Errands to the office, opening difficult windows, and carrying things from my car to the classroom were just a few of the extra chores. My students also helped the custodians, lunch monitors and office staff. These opportunities provided the students with variety, physical movement, change of scenery and the gratitude of many people.

Assign a younger or less capable student to a student with behavior problems: Giving students with behavior problems responsibilities is an effective way to help build their self-esteem. The responsibility, perhaps most effective, is to assign a student to assist a younger or less capable student. The student with behavior problems so often is the one who requires extra help, which is a painful reminder that he is different and needs help to meet the level of his peers. Reversing this situation and allowing these students to be the one helping lets them know that you trust them with responsibility of this nature. Assuring them that you feel they have something to give is a terrific confidence booster. I know that many teachers are wary of sending a student, who sometimes seems to be "out of control," out of the room to help others. It has been my experience that with the right groundwork, these students seldom let us down.

At one point in my career I was called in on a consult for a second-grade student who had behavior problems. This was a boy who was very bright but also very disruptive. The other students in the class had begun to tease him. He responded with hostility and at times struck out physically. After talking with his teacher, I could see that she was close to her limit with him. I suggested sending him to the kindergarten room once a day for 10 minutes to "help" the kindergarten teacher with her class. The suggestion was met with immediate resistance. There was concern that he would hurt the younger children and be of no help and also that this would be an imposition on the kindergarten teacher. After some cajoling and arranging, the boy's teacher agreed. Everyday, the student would help escort the kindergarten class to the bathroom. After a few weeks I checked in on how the boy was doing. As I spied on the class I observed him bending down over the foot of a little girl tying her shoelace. He was gently explaining the importance of not walking around with untied shoes. The kindergarten teacher reported that the student was no problem and that he indeed was helpful. The boy's teacher reported that his aggressive behavior in the classroom greatly diminished. And so the plan was continued for the remainder of the year. It was just perfect for this student, boosting his self-esteem and giving him a break and change of venue.

Assign an older peer to spend time with the student with behavior problems: Students with behavior problems sometimes behave in ways that may be undesirable to their peers and as a consequence they have few friends. This is problematic since a major portion of our social skills is learned through peer groups. Students with behavior problems may know the rules of adult society, but without friends, they are unfamiliar with the social rules among children their own age. This can be a great disadvantage. A student who wears jeans even a half-inch shorter than the rest of the students in class can be socially stigmatized. Students with behavior problems miss out on even more crucial social rules. It is for this reason that I recommend assigning an older peer to "buddy up" with a student with behavior problems. The purpose of this type of pairing should be primarily for socializing. Assigning an older student to tutor a student with behavior problems is not the same thing as pairing the two together so that they can just "hang out." Most students with behavior problems need to learn how to "hang out." Eating lunch together, playing a game or sport, or just talking could have immeasurable benefits for both students. The student with behavior problems gets a positive role model, someone to talk with, and, best of all, a friend. The buddy student gets the rewards of being a sensitive and helpful person and, in the best of all circumstances, gains a friend as well. A word of caution: Do not assign an older buddy who is socially inept who also may be oblivious to the social rules of the peer group.

Display positive verbal and body messages: Classmates may scapegoat another student because they sense that the teacher doesn't like the student. Teachers who are verbally sarcastic or who make fun of certain students are, in essence, giving the other students permission to do the same.

Communication

Students with behavior problems are hypersensitive to criticism and often misinterpret what is said as being a rejection. For this reason it is important to be aware of the way you are talking and communicating with these students, whether it is criticism or not. Keep instructions simple and direct. Many students with behavior problems who engage in disruptive actions may be unaware of their behavior or unaware that the behavior is disruptive. Attempting to verbally respond constantly to all of these disruptions, the teacher would be talking quite a bit and the response would be interpreted as nagging. For students with behavior problems it is likely that the only verbal recognition that student would receive would be for disruptive behavior. Of course this doesn't mean to ignore such disruptions. Instead, whenever possible, use non-verbal cues. A tactile message such as a hand on the shoulder works well with some students. Sometimes visual signals, such as a wink, also work well. I worked out a series of private visual prompts with some of my students; no one else in the class knew about them. For example, when I rubbed my temples it signaled to a particular student that he was drumming on his desk and that I wished him to stop. Since it is nonverbal, this prompt can be done without the need for the teacher to stop instruction.

When verbal cues are needed, go directly over to the student. Do not give directions or re-direct students from across the room. Administrate consequences in a calm manner. Getting angry, yelling or humiliating students with behavior problems almost always will have a negative impact on the situation. The student could become confrontational or hostile in an effort to "save face" in front of peers.

The Indirect Approach

If you need to talk to a student with behavior problems about a topic that he will find unpleasant, it may be best not to take a "head on" tactic. No student wants to hear how badly he is doing or about his transgressions. It is even more difficult for the student to deal with these issues when the student is forced to have eye contact with the adult while being reprimanded. And, it is awkward for the adult when talking to a student and he doesn't give you eye contact. I had several ways of dealing with this. When I had to talk to a student about something that was unpleasant, I always tried to make sure that there was no one else around. I then would set up a situation where eye contact was not required. I played cards with the students, I ate with them, or I walked in the halls with them. All these activities do not require eye contact.

My favorite tactic was "the stapler method." In a corner of a room you can set up a stapler station which includes two staplers and piles of papers that "need" to be stapled. Talking with a student while you are both stapling is wonderful because the eye-contact problem is eliminated. If you hit a nerve, the student can hit the stapler a bit harder. Another favorite method is "the box in the car." I used this method when a student was somewhat angry or upset with me. I kept a heavy box in my car that had nothing important in it (i.e., old magazines). If a student was upset I would ask him to help me bring in the heavy box from my car into the classroom. This served several purposes — it gave the student a break from the classroom and a chance to move around. Dialogue often began while walking to the car and continued throughout the process. Most importantly, with this method the adult and the student work together to achieve a mission. The box can remain in the classroom until you need another little chat, but this time inform the student that you have a heavy box that you need help with carrying to your car. You can use the same box all year long.

Confrontation

There will be times when a student with behavior problems will need to be confronted about some inappropriate action. Make sure you are prepared for the confrontation. Consider these things:

1. *Know why you are being confrontive. What do you want to accomplish?* If the answer is a change in a specific behavior, then proceed. If it's to get something off your chest or to deal with your own anger, stop and rethink it. You are probably not emotionally ready to talk to the student yet.

2. *Be ready to ask the student how he sees the situation.* This question is important! It is necessary to understand his point of view and to remove your

own assumptions that may not be correct. Sometimes there is just a simple communication problem. You do not want to barrel into a situation until you know all the facts. It is important for the student to express his feelings and to have them validated. This assists the student in opening up and dealing with the event or situation that has occurred. It also reduces the chances that a student will shut down or become defensive and angry.

3. *Be ready to inform the student how you, the adult, are affected by the situation.* Students need to understand that, as another human, the teacher's emotions and concerns are valid.

4. *Have an idea how you are going to ask the student to change.* Consider your tone of voice, facial expressions, etc. Your message may be a positive one, but if your body language and voice are negative you will put the student on the defensive, which may defeat the whole purpose of the discussion.

5. *Have an opening statement that does not accuse.* Using an "I" statement, state a common positive goal (e.g., "I want to decrease the noise level in the room"). Point out some of the student's positive qualities (be sincere). Inform the student that you like him, but that you do not necessarily like all his actions.

6. *Be ready to explain how you would like to see the situation improved and why.* Ask the student if he has any ideas on how to improve the situation. If appropriate, offer a possible solution or solutions to the conflict. Coming to a meeting of the minds will help ensure cooperation.

7. *Choose the right time for the confrontation.* It is not ever going to be a good idea to talk to a student about getting along with his classmates five minutes after that student was dragged into the office for fighting on the playground. An angry or humiliated human stops taking in information accurately. You need to wait until the student is capable of hearing the message.

8. *If you use humor, be careful not to be sarcastic or cutting.* Do not use humor as a weapon. This may cause a student to become sarcastic as well, or in some cases, become verbally or physically aggressive.

9. *Rehearse the confrontation (use role-playing, etc.).* Consider how you will respond to a variety of reactions on the student's part. It doesn't hurt to practice in front of a mirror or colleague.

Pre-Setting

Students with behavior problems tend to do poorly during transition periods or when the routine or schedule is changed. They require advance notice and help in preparing for changes in activities and routine. Talk with the student about what items he may need for the next activity. If it is an activity that is unpleasant (i.e., a difficult social studies test), talk with the student about his feelings. It's a good strategy to have the student repeat behavioral expectations to the staff. This should be done on an individual basis as opposed to giving directions from across the room. Students with behavior problems are less likely to be anxious and disruptive if they have advanced warning about a situation change. It also is useful to have the student start thinking of strategies to use in a new situation before he is actually in the new situation. The opportunity to role-play several possible action strategies will help students learn to consider the consequences of different reactions to the same situations.

When transitioning to activities that the student has had trouble dealing with in the past it may be useful to do the following:

1. Ask the student to tell you two things that would be good to do during the activity.

2. Ask the student to tell you two things that would not be good to do during the activity.

3. Ask the student to tell you a plan of action he may have if he is having difficulty.

Charting and Documenting Behavior

Charting and documenting behavior also is important. In the course of actual "living in the classroom" it is very easy to lose your perspective. Obtaining a "baseline," or measurement of the student's behavior before intervention, will allow you to better determine whether the intervention is succeeding. As an example, if you have a student who continually calls out, you may want to reward the student with five minutes of computer time for every 15 minutes that student is able to control calling out. This intervention may work for the next 27 school days, but if that student comes into school on day 28 and calls out from the time he steps off the bus in the morning until the time he steps back on the bus after school, the tendency is to feel that the plan is not working. If you have charted the progress of the intervention, you will quickly realize that the student is just having a bad day. If the calling out continues after several days then it would be appropriate to consider modifying the intervention plan.

Another reason to document in the school setting is to provide evidence that a particular student may need more support. No administrator likes to see a hysterical teacher run into his office yelling "Get him in the resource room! He's driving me crazy." It is important to document the actual behaviors, the interventions you've tried, and the results of the interventions. In fact, most special education referral processes require documented information before the referral will be accepted.

Documentation and charting does not have to become a major project. I used a simple daily documentation sheet listing the names of all my students, with room to write two or three lines under each name, each day. If there was a problem I tried to write down what happened before the problem, what the problem was, the consequence, and the results of the consequences. If something good happened I wrote that down too. It took me about 7 to 10 minutes to write the documentation sheet for 12 to 14 students. I also used the chart to help my students see patterns. If a student asked to be mainstreamed into lunch, I would pull out the documentation book and review with the student the past entries for three weeks. We would decide together if we thought the time was right. If the student was not ready we would set a date in the future to review the book again. It was quite effective.

Chapter Five

Home Environment

The fact of the matter is that being a parent is hard work. It is an emotional, physical and sometimes even a spiritual journey that requires careful planning, support and, most importantly, a sense of humor.

Educators can play a vital role in assisting parents in creating a positive home environment. Many of the strategies used in the classroom can be modified and can be useful at home. Teachers have many responsibilities so it can be difficult to find the time to do everything and working with parents can be extremely time-consuming, yet when a good relationship is forged between the school and home the results are usually beneficial for the educators, the parents, and most importantly, the student.

It is, at times, difficult for the educator to talk with parents about the inappropriate behavior of their children. Discussions need to be sensitively addressed so that the parent does not feel threatened and does not become defensive. As a teacher, it was my policy to make the first discussion with a parent a positive one. (For some of my students that meant calling their parents on the first day of school.) It's important to be clear, direct and non-judgmental. It's best to talk about a specific behavior, such as, a student's difficulty in completing assignments. Avoid making sweeping statements such as, "Johnny is lazy." This may put off a parent.

Even in the best of all possible relationships between school and home there is the possibility that problems can arise. Something important to keep in mind is that just as it is unreasonable for parents to expect the teacher to be able to do everything they may ask him to do, it is just as unreasonable for the teacher to expect the parents to be able to do everything the teacher asks them to do.

It will be helpful for the teacher to keep in mind that being a parent is not an easy job. Many parents feel the task of raising children is like walking the high wire without a net. There are so many decisions to make, small and large. Parents often find themselves wondering if they are being too strict or too lenient, and they may ask themselves such questions as the ever popular, "If Susie's mother is letting her go, should I let my kid go too"? Sometimes there is more than one acceptable answer and sometimes there is no answer at all. The fact of the matter is that being a parent is hard work. It is an emotional, physical and sometimes even a spiritual journey that requires careful planning, support and, most importantly, a sense of humor.

Raising a child can be an extremely challenging yet rewarding experience. Dealing with a child with behavior difficulties can be more challenging, requiring a great deal of thoughtful planning on the part of the parent. Educators can remind parents of two key elements — try to keep your cool and try to keep a sense of humor. Children count on their parents to be in control. Although that may not always be possible, the parent needs to learn what to do to stay calm. Sometimes it may be necessary to take a break, a walk, a run, a bike ride or any other activity. Activities are great ways to blow off steam appropriately.

Every parent at one time or another feels that they are not in control of the situation. Often parents are frustrated because they simply don't know what to do. It's at these times that the high wire begins to shake. Knowing that there is a reliable and considerate educator who can assist is beneficial for the parent — it's the safety net under that high wire.

At home, as in the classroom, there are two ingredients that need to balance with each other — consistency and nurturance. To explain what that means requires some deeper understanding of each concept. Again, the educator can provide support for parents in these key areas.

Consistency

Consistency and structure encompass several components — limit setting, rules and follow-through. It is much easier to provide this type of environment in a classroom than in a home but not impossible. Not only will children feel more comfortable in this environment, parents also will. Consistency eliminates the need for parents to "reinvent the wheel" every time there is a problem.

Most children and adults too, respond best in a predictable environment. When individuals feel that they are *not* in control, then they try to control everything. Parents often notice their child's behavior becomes difficult when the routine is disrupted. That's why family vacations can be so harrowing or when visitors are staying over children become cranky. Routine is developed through the structure of daily living, which is why it is not always possible to provide as much consistency as is necessary. I have heard many people say, "life often gets in the way of our plans." Things happen that we cannot always predict or plan.

Setting Limits

It's a comfort to a child to know someone responsible is in charge who will not let things get out of control. (However, do not expect any child to admit this!) The child must be clear on "how far" he can go. If there are not any limits he will not have any idea when to stop and this can lead to some significant disruptive behavior. Setting limits can be a difficult task because we don't always know what the limits should be. It requires some introspection.

First parents need to know their own limits. For example, consider the parents' tolerance level for dealing with a whining child. Is their tolerance level limited to 5 minutes of whining or 20 minutes or no whining at all? Once parents know the answer to that question they must figure out realistic and acceptable expectations for their child. Is it reasonable to expect your child to whine for 5 minutes or 20 minutes or does the situation call for no whining at all? The parent also must take into account the situation in which the behavior is occurring. Tolerance levels will change depending on where the parent is, what time of day it is, and other factors that affect behavior.

Rules

Rules should be clear and direct. The child should understand what he is supposed to do and why he is supposed to do it. Rules should be reasonable and achievable. Parents sometimes set up their child for failure by asking him to do things which he may not be capable of doing (e.g., expecting a 5-year-old child to sit in Uncle Harry's living room for more than half an hour watching vacation slides of Egypt). The child should have a voice in making the rules. Just like adults children will be more prone to adhere to rules that they helped create. It is important that everyone, adult and child, feels they have some control. For one person to have all the power is never a good idea. Others start to feel resentful and may become oppositional. If a parent has all the power the child learns not to approach the parent to get his needs met because he feels that it's a waste of time and a useless venture. But, giving the child all the power can be dangerous for a number of reasons. Children do not always use the best judgment; they also need to learn to seek adult advice; and, a child who expects and demands everything to go his own way all of the time is impossible to live with. The parent could become a hostage as the child resorts to physical and emotional blackmail to get what he wants. ("If you don't get me this toy I'm going to scream and yell as loud as I can in this very public place.") Additionally, this does not prepare a child to become a cooperative member of society.

In reality no one gets their own way all of the time. Children need to learn how to state their needs, negotiate for what they want, compromise when necessary and deal with the outcome of the situation. If a child learns and uses these skills he will have a greater chance of living a successful life.

Follow-through

Follow-through on consequences often is difficult for parents. It is important for educators to help parents understand that if rules are broken there must be a consequence or these rules will be broken again. This is also true for rewarding appropriate behavior. If an agreement is made between a child and a parent for a reward for certain behavior the reward must be given if the child lives up to his end of the bargain. When follow-through is non-existent, or inconsistent, children learn not to trust the parent or worse, not to take the parent seriously. Once children lose trust in a parental figure it becomes difficult for them to trust other adults in their lives. This could include educators who make academic and behavioral demands on the children.

At times it is difficult to follow-through. Parents may feel that their children will hate them if they deliver a consequence, and children may reinforce this feeling by actually saying it in hopes of getting what they want. Sometimes parents may feel that it's not worth the effort or energy to follow-through with specified consequences for inappropriate behavior. The problem is that children will learn they can get away with things that they are not supposed to do and this will become the norm for the child. If the rule, for instance, is that the child has a 9 o'clock bedtime on school nights, then that is the time the child should go to bed (unless there is an extraordinary circumstance, the parent should stick to this time). If the parent allows his child to dawdle or if there is always a reason why the child cannot get into bed by 9:00 p.m., he will learn that there really is no set bedtime and the bedtime becomes as late as the child can get away with before the parent loses patience.

Becoming lax on follow-through can have several negative effects on parents. Parents eventually get tired of fighting with their children and sometimes give up entirely. This can create a disruptive and sometimes dangerous environment for children who, without the proper guidance and supervision, may act out of control. A parent also could build up resentment and hostility toward their child causing the parent to lose control. Children can be cooperative, but it is the parent who has to take the lead. If a parent is fair and follows-through this will be exactly what the child learns.

When parents follow-through, their job as a parent becomes easier. When parents "stick to their guns" the child eventually will learn not to argue knowing that the parent means business and no amount of pleading, begging, whining or yelling will change the decision.

Nurturance

When parents nurture their children they are showing them love, care and attention. It is this unconditional love that tells the child, "I may not always like your actions or behavior, but I will always love you, no matter what." A nurturing home provides a safe haven for the child where he can be who he is without fear of harm or humiliation.

Essentially, nurturing is the parents' way of taking care of their child, supplying the things that the child needs to grow — love, food, shelter and encouragement. A key element for parents in this process is accepting and validating their child's feelings by giving him opportunities to state his hopes, dreams and fears.

As with everything, a balancing act is usually required for a parent to be successful in nurturing his child. Every child is different and will require different things. As an example, think about a child's first visit to the ocean. Some children will be afraid to go into the water so the situation would require the parent to find a way to reassure and "ease" the child into the water. The parent could venture into the water first, then he could carry the child in, and eventually, the child could walk in while holding the parent's hand and, finally, the child would walk in independently. However, some children, upon seeing the water for the first time, may run in recklessly unaware of the potential danger. The nurturing parent must take a different tack with this child, by slowing him down and demonstrating how to enjoy the water while respecting the potential danger.

If parents find that it sometimes is difficult to nurture their child the educator should reassure them by letting the parents know that they are not alone in having these feelings. Children take a great deal of time and energy. They often are self-absorbed and demanding and don't always recognize their parents' emotional or physical limitations. Children can be all consuming. When a parent has been up night after night with a child who is suffering with an earache, it is normal to want to escape the house, run away, and join the circus.

Parents cannot be all things to their children at all times. It may be necessary to take a break or seek help and support from others. This does not mean that the parent is inept. It simply means that the parent is human. Turning to trusted educators, friends or siblings who have children of the same age can help since most other parents have gone through similar experiences.

The Consistency/Nurturance Combination

Now that the essential ingredients to good parenting have been discussed, here is the dilemma. Consistency and nurturance do not usually go hand in hand. People who are highly consistent and structured without being nurturing also may be rigid, distant or even unrelenting. This causes children to become resentful of these adults or, worse, afraid of them. And then again, people who are nurturing but are unable to be consistent can be too permissive. These are people who say things like, "Okay, I'll give you one more chance," after 15 chances already have been given. As a consequence children learn that the rules won't be reinforced and so they learn not to respect the rules.

A balance of consistency and nurturance is required to provide a supportive and predictable environment. Every parent should ask, "What am I weakest in, consistency or nurturance"? Educators can help parents identify their weak points and then parents can begin to work on those aspects.

Children who are experiencing behavior problems often improve when their environment is modified. The following are some home modifications that may be useful.

Teaching independence: Nurturing children can be a tricky business. Even though parents consider children the most precious thing on earth, at times it is difficult for them not to make mistakes. Every parent makes mistakes. Problems can arise when a parent who is attempting to nurture his child suffocates him in a blanket of over-protection. Children rely on parents to provide a safe space in which they can explore and become independent beings. Sometimes, though, we mistake a child's attempt to be independent as disrespect. It is important that parents allow their children to develop skills that will help them feel confident and secure. This requires taking the child's lead and going at his pace. It is necessary for parents to give their child the freedom to try new things while recognizing that the mistakes he makes are a way of learning, and an approximation toward a goal.

Role modeling: Parents demonstrate nurturance to their children by role modeling appropriate ways to express feelings. When a parent makes a mistake he has the opportunity to role model for his child how to correct that mistake, first, by admitting that he made a mistake, second, apologizing for it and then, rectifying the mistake to the best of his ability.

The affection parents show to their children and to others will have an important impact. Remember that the child may not always hear what the parents are saying, but they most often see what parents are doing. Finding common ground with a child, sharing human experiences and emotions will teach him how to make his way in the world.

Communication: The way in which a parent communicates also has a great effect on children. Speaking and communicating in a respectful manner teaches the child to do the same. Parents should never talk down to a child. It is essential for the parent to listen when the child is talking and to really hear what he is saying. Providing appropriate feedback in a manner that does not embarrass or humiliate the child will allow him to listen to the parent. A parent must give his child the option to intentionally make mistakes and to take the consequences without a sermon. If the child is too upset to talk about something, the parent needs to give him the time and space he may require to cool down so he can talk rationally. It helps to choose a non-emotional time for a discussion on a difficult issue. There may be times, as well, when the parents will need to do the same for themselves. When the topic is unpleasant for the parent it may be best not to charge on through. No child wants to hear about how badly he is doing or about everything he has done wrong. As I mentioned earlier, it is even more difficult to deal with criticism when the child is forced to give eye contact to the adult while being told of his inadequacies. Setting up a situation where eye contact is not required is a good idea.

Parents need to talk with their children at times and places when they are not feeling threatened. Raking leaves, shopping in the mall and other activities are all suitable times and places for talking with a child about sensitive issues. I had a father tell me that the best time to talk to his son was when he was driving on the highway. He told me, "He doesn't have to look at me, but he sure isn't going anywhere." (Review previous discussion about communication.)

Increasing self-esteem: Children with behavior problems seem particularly vulnerable to having low self-esteem. The best way to combat this is to start building confidence in children before these negative feelings start. This often can be done at home. Also an educator should encourage parents to get their children involved in activities that increase self-esteem.

Assigning responsibilities: There are always a million chores to be done at home and I believe that children with or without behavior problems should have a part in doing them. As in the classroom, chores at home are wonderful for the child with behavior problems. They provide a variety of activities and they help make the child feel capable and responsible. A child could do chores such as throwing clothing into a hamper, putting away toys, and carrying dirty dishes to the sink. Other jobs and chores could be discussed with the children at a family meeting.

The parent may or may not decide to give an allowance. In any event if the child does jobs or chores above and beyond the call of duty the parent may want to reward the effort with a special outing, time alone with the parent, or the parent could ask the child what he would like.

Working with younger or less capable people: Perhaps the most effective responsibility is having a child work with children or adults who could use assistance. This could be beneficial for younger siblings or relatives. Also a child could volunteer at a nursing home, an animal shelter, or any number of other community organizations. Again, like the classroom situation, it is often the child with behavior problems who needs the extra help. Reversing this situation and letting the child know that he is trusted and has something to give, is a terrific confidence booster.

Spending time with an older peer: If there is an older peer, neighbor, or relative a child admires the educator could suggest that the parent promote a relationship between the two. The parent could encourage the two to spend time together; invite the older child over, or invite him to join the family on an outing. The older child will provide a good role model to the younger and they both may have a good time! Children with behavior problems can be "turned around" by positive friendships.

Siblings: In most families siblings tend to argue and fight. This problem is sometimes elevated when one or more of the siblings has behavior problems. In the heat of the battle the child with behavior problems may become totally unreasonable. Parents must teach both the child with behavior problems and the child without how to handle these situations. In most family situations "the squeaky wheel gets the grease." Children with behavior problems can be very squeaky and the sibling who does not have behavior problems too often does not get enough attention. Additionally, there will be times when family outings or events have to be altered or canceled because of the disruptive sibling. This can be very difficult for the other sibling who then may begin to harbor resentment and anger at the sibling with behavior problems. Educators can explain to parents that these feelings of anger and resentment should be validated. They are real and reasonable feelings. If the parents can, they should plan some special time with all siblings, both individually and together. Ultimately, how a parent deals with difficult behavior will affect how all children in the family deal with it. For instance, if a parent is a screamer chances are that one or all of the children in the family will likely become screamers too.

Company and visitors: If visitors are expected parents must warn their children so they can adequately prepare. Educators can talk to parents about respecting the child's space at home — space that is important and private. The child may want to put away special items, especially if other children are coming. The educator can instruct the parents on how to help their child organize thoughts to make the preparations. Reminding the child, "The Smiths are coming with their 2-year-old so you may want to put your model airplanes away," is often useful to the child.

The child may get agitated or overly excited if there are children coming over. Unfortunately this may lead to inappropriate behavior which upsets the visiting children. Again, the parents can be instructed to sit down with their child and talk out strategies for a successful visit. Parents can rehearse with their child how to ask others to play and they can act out possible situations and talk about how to handle the visit.

Preparing the child for school: Parents should be encouraged to be as communicative with the school as possible. Things will work much better if the parents and the educational staff work together. It is reasonable for parents to request daily or weekly progress reports as appropriate and when the parents have concerns they should be encouraged to let the teacher and school staff know.

There may be times when the parents and the school disagree on certain methods or issues. Sometimes disputes can be serious and even painful. However, it is important for the child to stay out of the "line of fire." The educator needs to help the parent understand that if a child gets the message that they, as the parent, have no faith in the school or that the school staff are not capable, the child may lose confidence in the school situation. One of the worst things that could happen is an undermining of the structure and limit setting provided at school. In these situations, children with behavior problems manipulate, pitting the school against parent and vice versa. This is a destructive situation where much can be lost. By explaining to the parents that it is vital that they support their child's effort to be cooperative at school, the educator increases the possibility that school life will be much easier for the child.

Vacations: Vacations can be really difficult for many different reasons. Everyone in the family has expectations of relaxation and good times. This can be devastating because stress and tension usually occur under these situations. For the child with behavior problems a new schedule, different bedtimes, different food arrangements and a general feeling of unfamiliar territory are disorienting and confusing. A child returning to school from a vacation that has been filled with frustration and inappropriate behavior often will have behavioral problems that may last for weeks.

Long car trips can be challenging but can be completed without complications. Parents should plan on making frequent stops and they should bring along games and other activities that can be used in the car.

Bedtime: A common complaint of teachers is that children who do not get enough sleep and come to school tired invariably have behavior problems in school. This is why it is important for educators to assist parents in dealing with bedtime routines and issues. As with almost all aspects of life, consistency is going to be essential for the child with behavior problems. To this end, it is so important for parents to try and have a set bedtime for their child and a set routine before bedtime. It also would be helpful to start doing less stimulating and quieter activities at least one hour before bedtime.

Sleeping can be problematic for children with behavior problems. I have had many parents complain that their children wake up extremely early and they have asked me for suggestions on how to keep them in bed longer. The answer is, you don't. Parents can set limits for what the child can do when he wakes up early. It would be fine for them to do art work, look at a video-tape with the volume on low, read a book or any other quiet activity that will not disturb the other members of the household. Specific rooms can be off-limits to them before a certain hour. It is important for parents to teach their child that even though they may be ready to start the day other people in the house may not be ready and that they must respect the needs of others.

Mealtime: As with sleeping, proper nutrition is an important part of a child's life. It has behavioral implications in the educational setting. Many children with behavior problems have problems with eating and mealtime. Mealtimes can be quite troublesome. As a child I was not always the happiest during mealtime. I felt very confined and it was a rare meal when I didn't ask to go to the bathroom. I was usually done eating before everyone else and would become frustrated by having to wait at the table with nothing to do. This made me particularly susceptible to being disruptive or to becoming over-reactive to my older sister when she teased me.

Parents need to consider carefully the seating arrangement at the table. They should try not to seat siblings together who do not get along. Establishing specific rules for mealtime can be beneficial but these rules should be acceptable to everyone.

Chapter Six

Interventions

We spend a considerable amount of time telling individuals what not to do and what to do. We sometimes forget to tell them how to achieve what we are asking of them or we take for granted that the individuals know how to achieve what we have asked of them.

Even in the best of all possible school and home environments, some individuals will require behavioral interventions. Whenever designing an intervention plan it is best to include the student in the process as much as possible. It is never too early for students to be in on the planning of how to make success more possible for themselves. As in rulemaking, most individuals will be much more willing to cooperate with a plan if they have been involved in designing it.

Behavioral interventions designed to be used in the school environment could be modified for use in the home and vice versa. In fact, interventions should be as similar as possible in both environments in order to provide consistency and to eliminate confusion for the child.

Negative consequences in any plan should fit the "crime," without undue harshness. Students should have consequences for inappropriate behavior, but the consequences should be well thought out and appropriate. Keep in mind that few people can go from 0 to 60 in one step. Look for the next step in the behavior chain — the next step from where the student is now. Always try to think of "the big picture" and what you hope to accomplish with the consequences. I implore anyone working with children to heed these words: Avoid using humiliation as a behavior strategy. There is no need for it! Even if you can get an individual to be compliant for the time being, the long-term effects of humiliation are horrendous. Humiliation further feeds the doubts already planted in the individual's mind. It will decrease self-confidence and cause anger and hostility. And, if other children see you humiliating a child, they will do the same. Try to avoid statements such as, "You're acting like a baby," "Can't you grow up," or "You're so hyper." Using "I" statements takes the focus off the individual and describes the behavior in terms of its impact on others. For example, you might say, "I get very distracted when you talk while another student is talking. Let Mary finish, then I'll listen to you."

Half the battle for some individuals is to come to some conscious recognition of their own inappropriate behavior: What it is, why it occurs, when it occurs, or what stimulates it. Adults and peers can help by providing cues and prompts. It is important that the delivery of the message be done in a firm, gentle and caring manner. Once the individual is aware of his inappropriate behavior he can begin to formulate a plan of action.

Common sense, empathy and consistency are important tools in dealing with inappropriate behavior. Using these tools helps keep us all on "our best behavior."

School Interventions

Dealing with classroom disruption requires an understanding of the classroom and teachers. It is necessary to understand what teachers think, believe, experience, and most importantly, the actions they take. It is as equally important to understand the ways in which teachers make meaning in the classroom (Zimmerman 1995).

Much of the judgment, knowledge and decisionmaking that teachers exercise are learning interpretations of their own experiences. "The study of teacher thinking is based in part on the assumption that the teacher refers to a personal perspective, an implicit theory, and a belief system about teaching and learning" (Clark and Yinger 1978, p.30). Teacher knowledge is a situated construction of social networks, a textually produced phenomenon (Nespor and Barylske 1991). Previous experience, environment and interactions with others formulate it. Based on judgments reached, teachers formulate theories about the practice of teaching that includes techniques of instruction and classroom management.

Some discussion of theories and how theories are put into practice would be useful in terms of understanding the thoughts and actions of teachers. Theories are "vehicles for explanation, prediction, or control" (Argyris and Schon 1974, p. 5). "When someone is asked how he would behave under certain circumstances, the answer he usually gives is his espoused theory of action for that situation. This is the theory of action to which he gives allegiance, and which, upon request, he communicates to others. However, the theory that actually governs his actions is his theory in use" (Argyris and Schon, pp. 6-7). Many teachers discuss their conceptions of teaching and say which overt (espoused) theories guide their actions when they teach. However, what they say may be in opposition to the way they act (Angulo 1988).

Interviewing and asking teachers what their theories of learning or behavior are might not yield an accurate picture of their teaching practices. "We cannot learn what someone's theory-in-use is simply by asking him. We must construct his theory-in-use from observations of his behavior. In this sense, constructs of theories-in-use are like scientific hypotheses; the constructs may be inaccurate representations of the behavior they claim to describe" (Argyris and Schon 1974, p. 7). Espoused theories and theories-in-use often are incompatible and an individual may be unaware of the discrepancy between the two.

Theories-in-use maintain a person's sense of consistency. They give order to a person's world. "When our theories-in-use prove ineffective in maintaining the constancy of our governing variables, we may find it necessary to change our theories-in-use. But we try to avoid such change because we wish to keep our theories-in-use constant. Forced to choose between getting what we want and maintaining second-order constancy, we may choose not to get what we want" (Argyris and Schon 1974, p. 17). When instruction is interrupted by students, "teachers occasionally considered alternatives [to their planned instructional process] but hardly ever implemented those alternatives" (Clark and Yinger 1978, p. 40). That is, for various reasons, teachers tend not to change the instructional process in mid-stream, even when it is going poorly.

Congruence is when an individual's espoused theory matches that individual's theory-in-use. "Lack of congruence between espoused theory and theory-in-use may precipitate search for a modification of either theory since we tend to value both espoused theory (image of self) and congruence (integration of doing and believing)" (Argyris and Schon 1974, p. 23).

The espoused theories and theories-in-use of teachers are shaped by many factors, both experiential and theoretical. Certainly, for teachers who have formal training, many of their stated beliefs (espoused theories) and practices (theories-in-use) are based on the education they have received. Additionally, the structure of school systems, schools and individual classrooms is influenced by educational learning theories. In turn, educational learning theory is influenced by the perceptions of those who have experienced the classroom environment. There have been numerous studies on the best methods of instruction. Some of these studies are concerned entirely with dealing with classroom disruptions. Other research, although not entirely concerned with disruptive actions, includes strategies for dealing with classroom disruption.

It is useful to review major learning theories that may influence or guide teachers. These theories will impact the instructional methods and social interactions that teachers have with students. Learning theories can be divided into three perspectives: behaviorist, cognitive and humanist. (Two other major perspectives, the psychoanalytical and biophysical models, have been omitted from this book, not due to their lack of importance, but due to the fact that methods deriving from these perspectives are seldom utilized in the classroom.) Each of the perspectives reviewed in this book defines classroom disruption differently and each prescribes different actions for dealing with disruptions.

Behaviorist Theory

General Principles

The major concepts in the behaviorist theory of learning are based on the stimulus-response-reinforcement paradigm in which human behavior is thought to be under the control of the external environment.

Behaviorists approach the study of learning by concentrating on overt behaviors that can be observed and measured. Behavior itself is seen as determined by events external to the learner. In behaviorist theory there are no thought processes or internal mechanisms on which to rely.

Stimuli elicit or cue particular behavior and by reinforcement of that behavior the stimulus — response relationship — is maintained. A stimulus is "any condition, event or change in the environment of an individual which produces a change in behavior" (Taber, Glaser and Halmuth 1967, p. 16). By rewarding a student for what the teacher considers "appropriate" behavior, the student will continue to exhibit that behavior. Unrecorded behavior, or behavior that results in punishment, will be extinguished.

B.F. Skinner's theory of operant conditioning is a classic example of a behaviorist learning theory. He described operant behaviors as voluntary behaviors used in operating on the environment (Skinner 1954). Skinner excluded subjective experience from his theorizing and discussed the manipulation of behavior through stimulation and reinforcement. He believed that we are controlled by our past experiences through reinforcement and punishment. The Skinner approach to instruction involves building stimulus-response associations by cueing learners to the nature of the response desired and by providing immediate feedback about the correctness of the response elicited, so that correct responses are reinforced and incorrect responses are extinguished. Shaping behaviors by using small steps and reinforcing correct responses increases learning. "By making each successive step as small as possible, the frequency of reinforcement can be raised to a maximum" (Skinner 1954, p. 94).

Disruption Defined under the Behaviorist Theory

In research studies using behaviorist theories and techniques, disruption is usually defined by the teacher. The overall goal of the teacher is, most often, to create a positive classroom environment (Zimmerman 1995). Overt actions that are targeted for behavior modification often are actions that disrupt the entire class and may include, but are not limited to: talking out, making unnecessary noise, being out of seat without permission, fighting, swearing and talking back to the teacher (Poteet 1974). Once the teacher targets the action for modification, various methods are used to extinguish what is seen as disruptive and to reinforce what is seen as productive. As a proponent of behavior modification techniques Bates, identified problem behavior and when to implement intervention techniques, "A behavior requires intervention when one of the following events occur: several independent requests for assistance are made with the same individual, the person is behaving differently than other comparison groups and when there have been dramatic changes in the person's behavior" (Bates 1982, p.3). Bates targeted more specific behavior, such as non-compliance, which he defined as a refusal to follow specific directions and a failure to respond quickly to requests, for behavior modification.

In one study, students were reinforced for arriving at class on time, for having materials to work on or study, for staying on task, and for interacting appropriately with staff (Adair and Schneider 1993). Behavior modification has been used in another study to attempt to control and reduce calling out (James 1990). Behavior such as hitting, kicking, biting, scratching, throwing an object that strikes someone, climbing on furniture, repetitive jumping, loud vocalizations, spitting, knocking down furniture, damaging objects, and touching others, were all identified as aggressive and/or disruptive behavior in other studies (Mace, Page, Ivancic and O'Brien 1986).

Strategies Used in Dealing With Classroom Disruption

Reinforcement

Reinforcement is a procedure that serves to maintain or increase a behavior. Positive reinforcement is the presentation of a stimulus, as a consequence of a response, and has the function of increasing or maintaining that response. This is sometimes referred to as "Grandma's law" — "If you take out the trash, I'll give you a cookie," said Grandma. A classroom teacher will reward student action they find desirable in an effort to have a particular student and other students repeat that action and actions similar to it. Money, affection, approval, smiles, and attention are all examples of typical positive reinforcers (Joyce and Weil 1986, p. 114). Chatting and teacher proximity also have served as reinforcers in dealing with spelling errors, temper tantrums, irrelevant verbal behavior, and baby talk in special education classrooms for emotionally disturbed pre-adolescents (Zimmerman and Zimmerman 1966). The ideal reinforcers are social in nature. Spending time with a favorite teacher or staff person can be extremely enticing to a student, particularly a student who craves attention.

Negative reinforcement is the response of an individual based on the escape from, or removal of, an aversive stimulus as the consequence of a response (Sulzer-Azaroff and Mayer 1977). Nagging is an example of negative reinforcement.

Punishment

To increase the likelihood of a desired behavior occurring or to deter undesirable behavior, punishment is introduced. School detention, loss of recess, and being scolded by the teacher or the school principal are examples of common forms of school punishment.

Token Economy

Token economy programs involve giving students points that they can later exchange for a reinforcement of choice (Smith and Misra 1992). A well-designed token economy is one that targets a behavior, or an approximation of that behavior, that is immediately and consistently reinforced by delivery of an adequate number of tokens. The token is any object or symbol that can be exchanged for a variety of tangible reinforcing objects or events (Sulzer, Azaroff and Mayer 1977).

Researchers have cited some of the advantages of token systems. They permit immediate reinforcement for the students in a class by means of a common object that individuals can use to obtain objects that they find desirable. Since tokens are like money, the behaviors can be brought gradually under the control of a powerful natural reinforcer. Since tokens can have a variety of back-up reinforcers they are not likely to lose their reinforcing power (Birnbrauer, Burchard and Burchard 1970).

An elaborate token economy system in a resource room at Prospect High School in Illinois was designed and the success of its use documented (Adair and Schneider 1993). A point system was modeled after the functioning of a real-life banking system. Points were awarded on the basis of students' successful completion of set-targeted behavior, such as arriving on time and staying on task.

Token economies can be used to promote some actions of students and to deter other actions. When students exhibit the targeted or desired actions they are rewarded by a token of some sort which can be used to obtain something that the students find valuable. If the token system is structured so those tokens can be lost for inappropriate behaviors, the occurrence of those behaviors also should decrease. If a token system uses a "token loss" component, the teacher must be very vigilant to assure that token loss is used correctly. He must be careful that the targeted inappropriate behaviors are not so overwhelming that the student has little hope of maintaining a positive "bank balance" of points.

Behavior Modification Tools — Records and Contracts

There are many different ways to provide reinforcement and there are a variety of charts and records that are wonderful and effective tools. Although behavior modification is not always the best intervention for some individuals, it can be highly effective for others. When using behavior modification systems it is extremely important to incorporate into the plan how to slowly remove the modifications when the individual is ready to exhibit appropriate behavior without the system. I have used behavior modification record sheets in my own class and I have strongly recommended them to teachers and other educational staff with whom I consult when I felt it was an appropriate intervention.

The following are two examples of behavior modification record sheets. The first example is designed for a younger student or a student who has limited control and needs a great deal of reinforcement. The second sheet is designed for an older student or a student who may need reinforcement only once or twice a day.

* * * * * *

Student _____   Date _____

Behavior Modification Sheet

	Act.1	Act.2	Act.3	Act.4	Act.5	Act.6	Act.7
1. Put things back where they belong.							
2. Keep hands to self.							
3. Follow Directions of teacher and staff.							
4. Remain quiet during work periods.							
5. Complete tasks.							

- Student should easily be able to do three of the five goals on the chart; the remaining two can be more challenging.

- Student gets a checkmark for each goal achieved during an activity.

- The chart should be read with the student after every activity. The student should respond with a yes or a no to each goal when asked if he was able to reach that goal.

- This should be done as soon as possible after each activity. This also may help the student transition to the next activity more easily.

- A daily and weekly award can be given.

- Reinforcing rewards for the student could be the following: spending "special time" with a staff person of student's choice, extra free time, computer time, or tangible rewards such as markers, crayons and food. In order to receive the reward the student should earn 80 percent of all possible checkmarks.

- Provide opportunities for the student to earn extra checkmarks. (For example, staying out of a fight at the next table might earn an extra point on either goal number two or number four.)

* * * * * *

Checkmarks

Name_____   Teacher_____

	MON.	TUES.	WED.	THURS.	FRI.
1. Respect your classmates and adults.					
2. Walk in the room and halls.					
3. Put appropriate effort into assignments.					
4. Be prepared for gym class.					
5. Complete homework for mainstreamed classes.					
6. Keep your hands to yourself.					
7. Respect other people's property.					

COMMENTS:

- Student should easily be able to do three of the seven goals on the chart; the remaining four can be more challenging.

- Student gets a checkmark for each goal he achieves during an activity.

- The chart should be read to the student before lunch and before he leaves for the day. The student should respond with a yes or a no to each goal when asked if he was able to reach that goal.

- If student gets all seven checks he should receive a small reinforcement reward (pencil, sticker, lifesaver or points toward a preferred activity).

- A weekly reward also should be given. Since it is possible to earn 70 checks, achieving 60 should qualify the student for the weekly reward.

- The student should be able to earn extra or bonus checks for exceptional behavior.

- The student also may keep a corresponding chart that can be compared with the teacher's at the same point in time.

* * * * * *

Writing and Implementing a Contract

Using behavior contracts also is a very effective way to set limits and provide structure for students who are having behavior difficulties. Writing and implementing a contract is somewhat complicated but a relatively easy thing to do. It is, however, often done incorrectly. I did a consult a few years ago for a fifth-grade student who was in a self-contained special education class program. The student was having difficulty in his mainstreamed classes. He seemed to me to be the perfect candidate for a contract. I asked the teacher if she would like to try one and her response was, "I did and it did not work"! I asked her if I could see the contract and she quickly went to his folder and pulled out a piece of paper. The piece of paper said the following: "I will go to my mainstreamed classes and behave myself." Only the student signed it. This is not a contract! It provided no reason for this student to change his behavior. I worked with the teacher on developing what I would consider a behavior contract.

A behavior contract is described as a "formal agreement between the client and other significant individuals who are affected by or who affect the client's behavior. These individuals include the counselor, teachers, administrators, parents, juvenile court workers, social workers, and the client's peers" (Hackney 1974, p. 23). Some objectives of a behavior contract may include: obtaining a commitment to change a behavior; clearly specifying the conditions necessary to effect a change; and, laying out the consequences of the change for all parties (Hackney 1974).

When a student is exhibiting classroom disruption, that student and the teacher, or other educational staff should come to an agreement about what actions are acceptable and what actions are unacceptable. Once this agreement is made, consequences for both acceptable and unacceptable behavior are delineated and agreed upon. Usually the student is rewarded for performing acceptable actions and punished for displaying unacceptable actions. It is hoped that the behavior contract will encourage the student to engage in the agreed-upon acceptable actions. Conversely, it is hoped that the agreed-upon unacceptable actions will cease.

The results of a study that documented the progress of a third-grade boy who exhibited behavior that included making noise, wandering around the room at will, use of inappropriate language and physical aggression directed at classmates, indicated that after the use of a behavior contract there was a significant decrease in the number of out-of-school suspensions for this individual student (Shier 1969).

Bates recommended behavior contracting as a behavioral strategy that ensures student involvement and clarification of program procedures. He described the behavior contract as a format for establishing mutual responsibilities of all persons who participate in a behavior-management program and felt that, "...by requiring signatures, a more formal commitment to conditions should result in more successful program efforts" (Bates 1982, p. 13).

"Besides providing a logical, self-directed approach to problem-solving, the contract system forces the student to assume responsibility for his own behavior" (Thomas and Ezell 1972, p. 31). The contract also provides a written record of the decisions made by the student and the course of action the student intends to pursue. The formal nature of the contract often acts as a motivational device not only for the student but for the teacher as well.

Some guidelines that are important to remember include the following:

1. Contracts should be written in a collaborative process with the student and the teacher and/or other educational staff and should be written in a positive manner. Be certain to state those positive qualities or skills the student has, and if possible, how those qualities can be used to enhance success.

2. Expectations should be clear, simple and specific.

3. Goals should be achievable and specific. Consequences should be reasonable and do-able. Just as negative consequences should not be unduly harsh, positive consequences should not be too grandiose. Help the child generate a list of possible reinforcers and negative consequences.

4. Try to get as many people as possible who are involved with the student to have input in the designing of the contract. Parents at the very least should be aware that contracting is being done.

5. Contracts should be tailor-made for each individual student.

6. After the contract has been written, set up a conference for signing the contract. This conference should be direct, but not harsh. At the conference, the student should be asked what support he would like in working to be successful.

7. The behavior contract should not be viewed as a punishment, but as an enhancement. Help the student see that contracting defines not only his appropriate behaviors, but the adult's behaviors as well.

8. All parties concerned should adhere to the terms of the contract. Reviewing the contract first thing in the morning, before anything can go wrong, may help.

9. Everyone should have a signed copy of the contract, including the student and the parent.

Below are two examples of behavior contracts designed for two individuals I had consulted.

* * * * *

James Smith
Behavior Contract

Positive Qualities	Areas of Concern
- Positive relationship with Ms. Jones	- Striking others
- Other students like him	- Inappropriate talking
- Can be charming and cooperative	- Inappropriate touching of others
	- Inappropriate behavior in halls and bathroom

Goals for Staff to Use to Assist James:

- Controlling his anger by providing alternatives to negative behavior.
- Providing incentives for appropriate behavior.
- Providing alternative space when necessary.

Goals for James to Achieve:

- Special time with staff of his choice.
- Extra privileges.
- Extra recess time.
- Special activities (i.e., cooking).

James is a boy who has many positive attributes. However, at times, he engages in behavior that is both disruptive and inappropriate. James can earn things that he finds enjoyable when he acts appropriately. There will, however, be consequences for negative behavior. When James is engaging in negative behavior the following steps will be taken:

1. James will receive a warning about the inappropriate behavior.

2. If the behavior continues, James will be asked to sit at a designated seat. He will be required to sit in this seat for no less than ten minutes.

3. If James is unable to maintain himself at the designated seat, he will be required to go to a designated spot out of the classroom for a period of no less than thirty minutes.

If James exhibits overt aggression toward anyone, he will be removed from the class immediately. He will be required to remain out for at least one hour.

Signatures:_____

_____

* * * * * *

Frank Doe
Bus Contract

Frank has been doing quite well in school this year. However, there have been some problems on the bus. In order to help Frank act in a safe and appropriate manner on the bus, the following terms of this contract should be agreed upon.

Frank will:

Follow the bus driver's directions.

Stay in his seat.

Keep his hands to himself.

Refrain from throwing objects on the bus.

If Frank is successful in abiding by these terms he will earn the following:

Time to play games (Legos™, cards, etc.).

(After 5 school days with no referrals)

Earn special time with a designated staff person.

(After 10 school days with no referrals)

Earn a lunch out.

(After 20 school days with no referrals)

Frank will earn these things at a designated time. We all hope that Frank can be successful and safe on the bus. However, if Frank is unable to improve his disruptive and dangerous bus behavior, he will lose the privilege of riding on the bus.

Signatures:

Student _____

Principal _____

Teacher _____

Parent _____

Bus Driver_____

* * * * * *

Modeling

Another intervention used for dealing with disruption in the class is the use of modeling through peers or adults. Behavior modeling is based on the concept that many behaviors are learned most effectively through modeling or imitation (Bandura 1965; 1969; 1971). For modeling to be successful, disruptive students would model either their peers or adults to elicit the desired actions.

Some individuals are more likely to imitate or model behavior from certain individuals, but not from others. For example, young male teachers have observed young boys imitating them by copying clothing or hairstyles. Little girls often model their teachers, particularly if they are women (Reinert and Huang 1987). It stands to reason that students will model a teacher whom they like rather than one they dislike.

Teachers should try to find positive students in the class that other students will follow and imitate. A student who is recognized by the teacher as being disruptive is encouraged to imitate a student who is considered to be cooperative. Modeling also can have the opposite effect such as when students imitate the disruptive actions of another student. This is often very frustrating for the teacher and is highly discouraging.

Oppositional Plans

When a student is continually defiant and constantly oppositional it's time for an oppositional plan. An oppositional plan is a step-by-step plan of action that involves giving the student choices of behavior. There are consequences for each step. Here is an example of an oppositional plan used for a student with behavior problems in a junior high school program.

Steps for Dealing with Oppositional Behavior

1. When John is exhibiting oppositional behavior (not following a reasonable direction), he should be given two prompts (20 seconds in between warnings).

2. If after the second prompt the behavior continues, John should be told, "You have a choice of following directions or going into the 'stress-free zone'," (designated spot), for at least five minutes. When the time is up, have John verbalize that he is ready to join the group and follow directions. If he is unable to do so, he should remain in the "stress-free zone."

3. If John refuses to make a choice, explain that you will make the choice and take him to the stress-free zone. If John refuses to go to the stress-free zone or goes and is disruptive, he should be brought to "time-out," (a spot outside of the classroom), for at least 10 minutes.

4. If John is not ready to join the group he should remain in time-out.

5. If John needs to go to the "stress-free zone" more than three times during a class period, the fourth time he should go to time-out.

6. John should have the option of requesting to go to the "stress-free zone" and should be encouraged to use this option when he feels himself starting to lose control.

Some behaviors may require placement in time-out immediately and without warning. Such types of behavior could include striking or hurting someone, throwing furniture or any behavior that is self-injurious or dangerous to others.

A request by the teacher or staff for John to go to the stress-free zone or time-out should be presented in a non-punitive manner. John should be made aware that everyone wants to see him happy and safe. Appropriate statements may include, "We're sorry you're having such a difficult time." "It seems you need some time away from the group." "We want to help you get yourself back under control so you can join us a soon as possible."

Cognitive Theory

General Principles

Cognitive theorists view learning as the acquisition or reorganization of the cognitive structures through which humans process and store information. The student is not passively reacting to stimulus, but is an active participant in the learning process. It is the learner's own information-processing capabilities that determine his learning and it is the teacher's job to develop ways to stimulate learners to use these capabilities to process the information to be learned (Bruner 1966; Gagne 1985).

Learning is an ongoing process of developing an increasingly sophisticated cognitive structure for representing and interacting with the world (Bruner 1966). The teacher's role, according to Bruner, is to, " . . . extend the student's range of experience, in helping him [sic] to understand the underlying structure of the material he is learning and in dramatizing the significance of what he is learning" (Bruner 1969, p. 9). Learning is considered to be information processing. "Once the stimulation from external energy sources reaches the human receptors, it is transformed by them into patterns that can best be understood as conveying information" (Gagne and Glaser 1987, p. 53).

When a child begins his educational experience he may not have the experience or knowledge of what social actions to take. This is particularly true if he has had no previous experience socializing with other children. The

53

teacher must provide an environment and present information that can enable that child to process the actions that could benefit him the most. The teacher should instruct students on the rules and try to provide an atmosphere in which students choose actions that are non-disruptive. A child who is not accustomed to taking turns must learn that in a school situation taking turns is essential in certain circumstances. The child who pushes ahead of other students at the water fountain will probably get some quick instruction from not only the teacher but from classmates as well. This information will be stored and processed and the next time the student is interested in getting a drink of water the course of action may be quite different (Zimmerman 1995).

Bruner discussed four themes of learning. The first theme is concerned with giving students an understanding of the "fundamental structure," (Bruner 1969, p. 11) of whatever subjects are to be taught. If students are to transfer knowledge to other areas, it is necessary to provide an understanding of fundamental structures which include not just teaching the mastery of facts and techniques, but the teaching of supporting habits and skills that make possible the active use of the materials learned. What is desired is assisting the student to reach an understanding of a "general idea," which then can be used as a basis for recognizing subsequent problems as special cases of the idea originally mastered. Children who learn to take turns at the water fountain hopefully will generalize that processed information and wait their turn in other areas such as on the playground.

The second theme focuses on Bruner's belief that "any subject may be taught to anybody at any age in some form" (Bruner 1969, pp.12 - 13). The key is to present information in a form that is at the student's readiness level. "The task of teaching a subject to a child at any particular age is one of representing the structure of that subject in terms of the child's way of viewing things" (Bruner 1969, p. 32). A teacher, then, must consider the age of the student and other factors that might affect that student's ability to comprehend the information being taught. "A curriculum as it develops should revisit basic ideas repeatedly, building upon them until the student has grasped the full formal apparatus that goes with them," (Bruner 1969, p.13).

The third theme encourages the use, by students, of intuitive thinking, which provides the training of hunches and educated guesses. The teacher should support ideas generated by the student that are based on "gut feelings," that derive from what the student already knows and is using in an attempt to solve problems, social or academic.

Finally, the fourth theme relates to how students can be stimulated and motivated to learn. Bruner recognized that although competition for high grades exists, he does not feel that this is the best way to motivate students to learn. Creating an interest in a subject is the most beneficial method for developing motivation to learn. The best way to do this is "to create interest in a subject by rendering it worth knowing, which means to make the knowledge gained usable in one's thinking beyond the situation in which the learning has occurred" (Bruner 1969, p. 31). Providing information and instruction to a student in a manner that enables the student to see that it is useful information, and relevant to him is essential. This also will reduce occurrences of disruptive behavior. Students who are engaged in meaningful activity seldom act out.

Disruption Defined under the Cognitive Theory

Cognitive theorists are concerned primarily with the process of learning and information acquisition. Since the student must be an active participant in this process, a student who simply refuses to participate would be considered disruptive. Students not open to the acquisition and processing of information may choose not to listen in class or to withdraw from the instructional experience. Students who process information but who choose not to use that information also may be considered disruptive. Disruptive actions would be considered those actions taken that are impulsive or actions taken without thought. The goal is for the teacher to present information to the student who in turn processes this information and uses it to formulate actions that are not disruptive. A student who is prone to losing his temper and to fighting would be encouraged to think before he acts (Zimmerman 1995). Many of the articles concerning metacognition target impulsive behavior (Huhn 1981; Larson and Gerber 1984; Meichenbaum 1971). Other actions targeted are on task behavior (Cameron and Robinson 1980), interpersonal problems (Meichenbaum and Asarnow 1987), and homework completion (Fish and Mendola 1986).

Strategies Used in Dealing With Classroom Disruption

Numerous applications of cognitive theory relating to disruptive classroom actions have been cited. Structuring and assisting students in the storage of valuable information concerning disruptive actions can be quite useful. Most cognitive theorists believe that one starts with the pre-existing knowledge students bring with them into the learning situation. From there the learner is brought from novice to expert (Nisbett, Fong, Lehman and Cheng 1987; Shuell 1990; Weinstein and Mayer 1986). In bringing the student to the expert level the teacher takes what the student already knows and assists the student in enhancing and expanding the pre-existing knowledge and strategies. In dealing with students, and teaching them to be non-disruptive, the teacher draws on what the students know about their own actions (what has been successful before, what makes them disruptive, etc.) and helps them to become more adept at dealing with social situations. Included in this process are the students' own reflections as they generalize concepts (Shuell 1990). Students working on strategies to reduce disruption may test out some verbalizations that they have acquired in different social settings. Hopefully, the students will see the relationship between acting a certain way and achieving a certain desired goal, and will ascertain if these strategies are useful. At the expert level, the students who have acquired strategies for dealing with disruptive actions use these strategies automatically when they encounter situations that cause them to be disruptive in the classroom.

Another application of cognitive learning theory to aspects of disruption is evident in Flavell's theory of cognitive monitoring (Derry and Murphy 1986, p. 9; Flavell 1979, 1981). This monitoring may include teaching learning tactics to students, helping students recognize learning goals, creating and building experiences that lead to learning and developing students' metacognitive knowledge of how and when to use learning tactics (Flavell 1981).

Metacognition

We spend a considerable amount of time telling individuals what not to do and what to do. We sometimes forget to tell them how to achieve what we ask of them or we take for granted that the individual knows how to achieve what we have asked of them. When an individual is frustrated and angry we may tell them not to yell or not to hit anyone. What we also need to tell him is how to deal with the feelings he is experiencing. Most individuals have a "little person" inside their head that helps them to monitor behavior. This is the little voice inside the student's head that reminds him to raise his hand before answering a question. For impulsive students this little person is tied and gagged and offers no assistance. The usual plan of action is impulse, first, then thought and then action. Many students with behavior problems go from impulse to action. This leads to some serious judgment flaws and inappropriate behavior. By giving these individuals coping strategies, we assist them in making positive choices. Although they may not choose an appropriate strategy, or any strategy at all, they must at least have the option of choosing.

In terms of classroom action the issue is how to teach students to discover and use strategies that will be successful in monitoring their actions. It is equally important to ensure that once these strategies are learned, they generally can be used in different situations. The idea is to teach the students strategies for planning and problem-solving in a way that will enable them to use their thinking processes to choose a plan of action that is successful or may be successful across a variety of situations and settings. What you really want the individual to do is to social-problem solve. Teaching children to talk to themselves (internally) to guide and mediate their behavior in a problem-solving manner gives them that structure. Students with behavior problems can be particularly sensitive to criticism. They can become over-reactive and even hostile when feedback is provided. This is sometimes the result of an unquenchable need for reassurance and acceptance, or simply the fact that they have seldom received any feedback that was negative in content. However, once the student is aware of the inappropriate behavior he can begin to formulate a plan of action.

Metacognitive theory deals directly with teaching students strategies that are useful for monitoring their own actions (Fish and Mendola 1986; Huhn 1981; Larson and Gerber 1984; Waksman 1985). Metacognitive processes are those processes that enable the learner to self-monitor and to direct his actions through the monitoring of his own thinking processes. Meichenbaum, who is a major proponent of using metacognition in dealing with classroom disruption, described metacognitive processes as including: (a) prediction and planning, which precede problem-solving attempts; (b) checking and monitoring, which are subsequently performed to evaluate the outcomes of these attempts; and (c) checking outcomes for internal consistency and against "commonsense" criteria (Meichenbaum 1971). In short, such processes as checking, planning, asking questions, self-testing, and monitoring ongoing attempts to solve problems are central components of metacognitive development. See the four-step program, below, for developing a useful strategy (Meichenbaum and Asarnow 1979):

1. The student needs to realize the need for a strategy.

2. The student has to evaluate the task requirements and then has to select from an array of routines that might be appropriate.

3. Having selected one, the student needs to execute the strategy and monitor its efficacy.

4. Monitoring efficacy provides feedback that would govern decisions about future actions.

Modeling procedures, behavioral rehearsal, role-playing, and other methods provide useful tools for teaching metaprocesses. From this perspective, the teacher's task is to provide the necessary instructional prompts by setting up situations in which the student can learn and practice newly acquired strategies. This process also requires the teacher to encourage problem-solving behavior or metacognitive development displayed by students (Meichenbaum and Asarnow 1979).

There is a need for teaching problem-solving techniques that would enable children to become sensitive to interpersonal problems and that would develop the ability to generate alternative solutions (Meichenbaum and Asarnow 1979). Also Meichenbaum and Asarnow suggest that students should be taught to understand means-end relationships and the effect of one's social acts on others. Children should be taught the distinction between facts, choices and solutions. A variety of teaching aids, cartoons, workbooks and poster-pictorial card activities are used to teach children to identify problems, to generate alternatives, collect information, recognize personal values, make a decision, and then review the success of that decision at a later time. Inherent in such an approach is the need for a careful task-analysis by both the teacher and the student. A task-analysis is a complete breakdown of all components of a task that would enable an individual to see at what point a problem may develop. The teacher also can use a task-analysis to determine whether the desired behavior includes skills not yet developed by the student, and thus requiring instruction.

Modeling actions in a social setting, a key element in metacognition, assists the student in understanding what actions to take (Fish and Mendola 1986; Huhn 1981). Joint participation in an activity permits cognitive processes to be displayed, shared and practiced, so that the child is able to modify his current mode of functioning (Vygotsky 1962). The teacher can model important metacognitive processes for the child while teaching skills, by breaking up the processes into smaller components that are easier for the student to handle. In this model, learning takes place at the "zone of proximal development." This zone is the space between a student's display of independent abilities and a display of these skills only with social support. An example of a student using metacognition to monitor actions might be a student who, when frustrated, verbalizes either out loud, or internally, strategies that have been taught for dealing with this frustration. These strategies may include breathing deeply or raising a hand and asking for permission to leave the room for a brief walk. Eventually, the verbalization diminishes as the student automatically employs the learned strategies for dealing with frustration.

Another example of the distinction of the zone of proximal development for teaching strategies might be a student who has difficulty walking alone in the halls without engaging in some disruptive action (i.e., yelling or running). The student is able to walk appropriately with one other student, but not alone. This is the place where learning takes place, or the zone of proximal development. A teacher may use some of the following methods to teach the student the cognitive skills which would enable that student to walk unescorted in the halls: rehearsal, self-verbalization (speaking to one's self and reviewing proscribed steps) and modeling of appropriate behavior in the halls.

Plans of action that can be used to get through difficult situations are essential for the student to be successful. By teaching students metacognitive and self-monitoring skills we give them a fighting chance in times of stress. Below are some guidelines for teaching students in metacognitive and self-monitoring skills:

Problem Recognition

It is important to teach children to understand and recognize different types of problems, and how their own actions can cause problems. Very often a student with behavior problems aggravates or annoys another student without even knowing it. Later in the day the aggravated student may "get even," leaving the student with behavior problems feeling confused and persecuted. It is useful to point out all factors that cause problems. Sometimes a sensitive peer, particularly one who likes the student with behavior problems, can help accomplish this end.

Self-monitoring

A good way to help students with behavior problems to be able to predict problems before they occur is to teach them to monitor their own thoughts, feelings and bodies; and to recognize the "signals" that indicate a "plan" should be used. Very often we feel things on a physical level before we feel them on an emotional level. (Some individuals breathe heavily and their face may turn red when they are angry.) Students can learn what these physical signals mean and use them to predict their own behavior. (As a corollary to this, students can learn to "read" the non-verbal behaviors of others to better predict other people's behavior.)

Solution Generation

Teaching students to generate more than one possible solution to a problem will help them be flexible. I had a student with behavior problems in my class who had a horrific time in the cafeteria. We worked on a plan for him to talk to the lunch monitor when things were rough. I had spoken to the lunch monitor to advise her that this was our plan. The plan worked fine until this particular lunch monitor was absent. When a problem came up the student, sticking to our plan, spoke to the substitute lunch monitor. Her response was to tell him to stop being a baby. He became enraged and furious at her and at me as well. If he had had an alternate plan, when the original didn't work, much pain and disruption might have been avoided.

Anticipating Obstacles

As noted earlier, life never goes smoothly, or how we expect it to, all the time. That is why it is important to teach children to think of new "plans" if they encounter obstacles. One can seldom anticipate every possibility before hand. Children with behavior problems should be encouraged to be creative when they encounter obstacles to previous plans. Helping them consider the set of possible behaviors tolerated by others and the set beyond other people's tolerance will help guide them as they choose alternatives.

Consequential Thinking

Every action causes a reaction. Children must learn to take responsibility for the actions they choose.

Visualization

Teach children to picture in their heads difficult situations in which they may find themselves, such as being in the cafeteria. Children should try and imagine all possible events and imagine strategies for these events. Spending five minutes with a student with behavior problems and having him mentally visualize a place of conflict can help to prevent problems. Mental imagery is similar to running a movie in one's mind, but in this case, it is a movie over which one has complete creative control. In a sense, it is a type of useful daydreaming. The key here is to decide in advance what the desired outcome is.

Relaxation

There are many methods of teaching children specific relaxation procedures and techniques. These are very useful for students with behavior problems who often have no idea how to calm down or relax. Telling them to calm down or relax is not enough. You must give them the techniques. A colleague of mind told me about a kindergarten teacher who taught his entire class basic yoga — everyone, including his students with behavior problems, gained focus and calmed down.

Dealing with Anger and Frustration

Teach children to seek alternatives to aggressive behavior when they are angry or frustrated. It would be a mistake to tell children not to be angry or frustrated, as this is sometimes impossible. However, they can request to talk to someone, take a walk, count to 10, take deep breaths, scrunch up their toes in their shoes, or any number of actions preferable to hitting or striking others. Using a classroom mediation strategy in which the entire class is trained to mediate disputes is often very successful.

Self-instructional Training

The ultimate goal is to have students with behavior problems learn to problem solve. However, you must provide the structure necessary for them to be able to do so. One way would be to teach students to talk to themselves (internally), to guide and mediate their behavior in a problem-solving manner. Children could ask themselves:

What is the problem?

What are some plans?

What is the best plan?

Have I tried this plan?

Did the plan work?

Reinforcement

Using these metacognitive and self-monitoring skills is hard work for the student with behavior problems. When students use plans as opposed to acting impulsively it is helpful to encourage and motivate them with positive reinforcement.

Academic Modifications

Many students who have behavioral difficulties have co-occurring conditions, most often learning disabilities. As a result some students may require many academic modifications and some may not require any at all. Often when a student's academic program is modified the student's behavior improves dramatically. Academic modifications should be tailored to meet the needs of the individual student. Modifying appropriately can be a difficult task. It is important not to modify or "fix anything that's not broken." Providing a crutch when it is not needed may cause students to believe they are worse off than they are or may create a dependency on an unnecessary crutch. Conversely, if modifications are not extensive enough the student often becomes frustrated and angry. This in and of itself can create behavioral difficulties in a student who, up until this time, had none. The following are some suggested academic modifications that I have used in my classroom or have suggested to others. I have broken them down into specific categories of academic areas.

External Scaffolding

Most people consistently organize thoughts and plans of action internally. An average child usually understands and follows the morning routine before a school day without needing a checklist in a written form. Information about the routine is stored in the child's memory and when they wake up they do the things they need to do (eat breakfast, brush teeth, comb hair, get books ready, etc.) and then they mentally check off these tasks. For some children, waking up in the morning can be a nightmare as the child feels overwhelmed and doesn't even know where to begin. This lack of internal structure can also cause a tremendous amount of frustration that may create a situation in which the child shuts down. Imagine waking up like this every day! Being prepared for the events of the school day and then living through the school day can be extremely difficult. The student can sometimes have one disaster followed by another and feel completely overwhelmed and inadequate. It is for these reasons that the student needs help in developing an "external scaffold." The external scaffold replaces or at least compensates to some degree for the student's inability to organize internally. Some children need just a light framework because they are able to organize some things internally yet others will require a great deal more. As the student begins to internalize some of the routines and responsibilities, the scaffolding can be reduced. For some students, however, this will be a life-long battle and they will require this scaffolding forever. Some strategies for creating external scaffolding are:

1. Teach the student how to make a list and how to follow it. People sometimes take for granted that making a list is easy while students with behavior problems have difficulty with this task and with following through. Start small (no more than two or three simple tasks on a list) and then work your way up to longer and more complicated lists. It may help to start by having the student create a list for a schedule he already knows and follows.

2. It is important that students with behavior problems understand and know how to follow a schedule. If you need to, start with an hourly schedule then work up to daily, weekly and monthly schedules. Students with behavior problems are notorious for asking, "What time is lunch?" at 8:30 in the morning. To these students it is a legitimate and sincere question, related to their poor sense of time. It is essential for success, in the present as well as in the future, for a student with behavior problems to use calendars, clocks and schedules as tools to help them follow the routines. A schedule taped to a student's desk can be very helpful. Children who have not yet learned to tell time will need a schedule with times and their representations on clock faces. Being able to follow schedules alleviates much of the stress that people with behavior problems have. They are aware of what is coming up and there are fewer surprises. I find

my schedule book, with its calendar, an extreme source of comfort and I am most unhappy and anxious without it. I take it everywhere.

3. Use a homework assignment chart and a classwork assignment chart. At first, filling out the chart will be the responsibility of both the student and the educational staff, but eventually the student should take over the responsibility. Students will differ in terms of how long it will take before they can assume this responsibility themselves.

4. Provide a binder that has several organized sections for work to be done, homework assignment charts and completed assignments. It also should contain daily and weekly schedules, and the names of people (where and when to find them) to contact when there are problems. Color coordinate the binders for easy access and insist that the student carry the binder with him at all times. Recognize that for a significant time period after establishing the folder system, adult cueing will be necessary to keep up with the folder(s).

5. Provide a set of materials to be used in the classroom and a set of materials that will be kept and used at home. Materials should include a writing implement, paper and any books the student may need. Emphasize that the materials used in school should not leave the classroom and the materials used at home should not leave the house. Many students with behavior problems are disorganized and disheveled. They have difficulty holding onto and transporting materials. This does not signal a lack of respect for materials, but an inability to remain focused on the possession of the materials.

6. It will be useful to break up larger assignments or projects into smaller components with specific deadlines for each component. Not only does this make a larger task less overwhelming, it provides a road map for tackling the project.

Teach a student with behavior problems how to ask questions and make comments appropriately. So often a thought or question pops into the student's head and he immediately shouts it out. Instruct by modeling what to do when you have a question or comment. (It is not a good idea, for example, to talk about how the puppy ripped up the couch in the middle of a science lesson.) The student needs to be told this and told what to do if he has a question or comment at an inopportune time. Suggest that the student write the question down for later, or if a tape recorder is available, to quietly tape the question. Keep in mind that one reason students with behavior problems shout out is that they know if they wait they may forget their comment or question. In any event, there should be consequences for students when they inappropriately blurt out things and there should be consequences when they successfully have controlled themselves. As previously stated, it is always important to reinforce appropriate behavior.

Some students would benefit greatly by doing assignments on a computer. The use of a laptop computer or a computer workstation could be helpful. Many students with behavior problems have considerable difficulties with handwriting. Using a computer reduces that problem, although keyboarding may be slow. It is also a motivational method since assignments tend to get done faster, and the student has the advantage of being able to edit and correct before turning in an assignment.

A multisensory approach to assignments can be quite useful. Fulfilling some assignments in an oral manner helps motivate students with behavior problems to do tasks such as homework. Creating a mural, a diorama or a performance piece that explains or includes elements of the concept to be learned is likely to result in greater learning and greater retention as well.

Physical Structuring

Seating assignments are extremely important. It is usually best to seat a child with behavior problems in the least distracting seat in the room and that usually means up front. When I was a student, even if I began the school year seated in the back of the classroom, it wouldn't be long before I ended up in the front row. It should be noted, however, that some students with behavior problems do better seated in the back. If, for instance, a student tends to squirm and move around in his seat distracting everyone behind him, then a seating assignment in the back of the room might be better for him. Some teachers assign two seats and allow traveling between the two for students who have movement needs. If possible, seat the student next to another student who will be a positive influence. Also, it's not a bad idea to change the seat every now and then to provide some variety for the student. How often a change will need to be made depends on the individual student. Provide an alternate, more isolated, spot in the room for a student to request or for the staff to request when concentration is particularly difficult. This option should not be presented as a punishment but as a tool to assist in completing tasks and projects.

Provide plenty of hands-on activities. This satisfies a need for movement and is motivating to the student. Alternate sedentary tasks with more lively activities. Try to get students with behavior problems up and about from time to time as part of an activity. Activities should be scheduled for no longer than 20 to 30 minutes. For younger students (kindergarten through second-grade), 10 to 15 minutes may be the limit.

Instructional Levels

The most effective academic "modification" really is not a modification, but the way *all* students should be instructed. That is, all students should be instructed in a range of 95 to 97 percent *known* material and no more than 3 to 5 percent *new or unknown* material. This means building on existing skills. When students are instructed at their *independent* levels (more than 97 percent known material, which should be used for only independent practice), they become bored and may become disruptive. When they are instructed at their frustration levels (94 percent of less known material), they become frustrated, tune out, and may become disruptive.

Humanist Learning Theory

General Principles

Humanist theory stresses the personal growth and interests of the individual student. Humanists emphasize the importance of understanding a student's perceptual world in order to help the individual fulfill his or her basic potential (Rogers 1983).

Instruction begins not only at the student's academic level, but where the student's interests lie. In his book *Summerhill*, A.S. Neill described his school program that is based primarily on the humanist learning theory. Neill attempted to "make the school fit the child instead of making the child fit the school" (Neill 1960, p. 4). At Summerhill classes were optional because Neill believed that when a child was ready to learn he would. Neill noted, "... we do not consider that teaching in itself matters. Whether a school has or has not a special method for teaching long division is of no significance, for long division is of no importance except to those who want to learn it. And the child who wants to learn long division will learn it no matter how it is taught" (Neill 1960, p. 5).

In order to make education relevant it is necessary to teach students in relation to the experiences that the students bring to school from their homes and communities. Many humanist theorists are concerned about the lack of relevance of instruction in school. "Often the material is not translated into life-terms, but is directly offered as a substitute for, or an external annex to, the child's present life. The following three typical evils result: 1. Lack of organic connection with what the child already has seen, felt and loved makes the material purely formal and symbolic. Without preliminary activities the symbol is bare, dead and barren. 2. Lack of motivation. 3. Even the most scientific matter, arranged in most logical fashion loses this quality when presented in external, ready-made fashion. It becomes "stuff for memory" (Dewey 1902, pp. 24 - 26).

Dewey felt that schools were not adequately utilizing the students' abilities and community experiences and that the education provided to students

65

was not useful in terms of the students' lives. "The great waste in the school comes from the student's inability to utilize the experiences he gets outside of school in any complete and free way within the school itself; while on the other hand he is unable to apply in daily life what he is learning in school. Natural connections should be made between the child's experience and education" (Dewey 1900, p. 75).

In addition, the humanist theory notes that the learning environment should be a place where students feel wanted, cared for and listened to. A display of real sensitivity and empathic understanding in the classroom is desired as "when you understand without judging, when you understand what it is like to live in the world of this other person" (Rogers 1987, pp. 40 - 41).

Many aspects of schooling bother humanists, particularly the school environment which they feel often does not provide an accepting atmosphere partly because the teachers are, at least in class, impersonal and boring. Many students, they believe, accept school as an unpleasant experience and discover that most of their relevant learning occurs outside of school (Rogers 1983).

Many problems in the classroom are related to the "assembly line" aspects of education, although most humanist theorists understand that the impersonal tactics in the classroom are difficult to change significantly because of cost, efficiency and traditions (Reinert and Huang 1987, p. 112).

The level of a child's self-confidence also plays a vital role in his education. In order for students to be successful in school it is vital that the student feel good about himself and his abilities. "With a true self-confidence, youngsters can explore and build on their innate curiosity. Youngsters who are encouraged to explore, to risk-take, to ask questions and challenge established assumptions are more likely to become creative and flexible adults" (Yau 1991, p. 157). Children should be nurtured and provided with a safe and secure environment. "Once a child feels truly secure, he/she is free to become an independent thinker" (Yau 1991, p. 160).

Humanist theorists stress the importance of social context. They consider the total child and the social world from which the child comes. In order to make the child's educational experience valuable, the social world of that child must be taken into account. This is another area where many humanists feel that schools are wanting. The use and knowledge of a child's social world to instruct that child is lacking — " . . .the tragic weakness of the present school is that it endeavors to prepare future members of the social order in a medium in which the conditions of the social spirit are eminently wanting. There is no sense of community. Schools are competitive and they foster an environment that makes cooperation bad" (Dewey

1900, p. 15). Dewey spoke about the weaknesses of many schools in the early 20th century, but, perhaps, the same can be said of many schools a century later.

Students who arrive into the school with "emotional baggage" have a particularly difficult time. "Schools are not successful in working with children in conflict. The child's home and community, which contribute to deviant behavior, often are ignored. More expedient areas of intervention, such as in-school punishments, are used instead of attacking the causes of the problem" (Reinert and Huang 1987, p. 112). School personnel generally have minimal training in sociological aspects of change. Programs designed to help those who are different often are funded on the basis of labeling thus encouraging the isolation of students who are disruptive (Reinert and Huang, 1987).

Montessori teaching employs some humanistic learning theories and promotes learning through feedback from the consequences of actions. "Learning should also occur in the social context of the classroom: children discussing their ideas of why something is not working" (Yau 1991, p. 155). This points to the fact that not only does the social world of the student need to be considered, but that the learning itself should be considered a social event.

Disruption Defined under the Humanist Theory

What is considered disruptive is what the individual or group finds disruptive. What is disruptive to one person is not necessarily disruptive to another. Because the humanistic perspective takes into account the individual as well as the group, the group generally determines what is disruptive behavior. What most certainly would be considered disruptive would be any individual not observing the established and agreed-upon rules of the class. Presumably, these rules would have been agreed-upon by the entire class (Zimmerman 1995).

A lack of respect of another's feelings, actions or property also would be considered disruptive. An infringement of any individual's rights would normally be seen as disruptive. At Summerhill, "each individual was free to do what he likes as long as he is not trespassing on the freedom of others" (Neill 1960, p. 155).

Anything that occurs in a classroom that would make an individual feel unsafe, unhappy or threatened also would be considered disruptive. These situations could occur in a physical form, such as someone striking someone

67

else, or in an emotional form, such as an individual being teased or humiliated.

Since feedback and interaction from the child are so important, anything that discourages students from speaking, for example one person interrupting another, is disruptive. Limited opportunity for students to speak would be seen as disruptive for a whole class or for individuals.

Strategies Used in Dealing With Classroom Disruption

For humanist educators a disruptive student is an indication that the student is unhappy or in conflict and in need of some attention. In dealing with students who are unhappy or in conflict, teachers should, humanists assert, treat these students in an empathetic way. This facilitates a situation in which students will be willing to talk and share their feelings. This may remove the need for a student to act in a disruptive manner due to an upset: "... if a person is being met with a sensitive, empathic understanding, he or she realizes that someone understands 'what it is like to be me.' That realization brings a whole rush of expressions of feelings. People are hungry to have someone else understand the persons that they are, and so you get more feelings about self. The feelings that are expressed in regard to self are increasingly relevant to whatever the conflict is" (Rogers 1987, pp. 43).

In a humanistic program, what is disruptive, or what potentially might be disruptive would be discussed with the entire group. Summerhill was a "self-governing school, democratic in form. Everything connected with social or group life, including punishment for social offenses, was settled by vote at the Saturday night General School Meeting" (Neill 1960, p. 45). At Summerhill the votes of the teachers and students were equal. Issues of what constituted "trespassing on others' freedoms" as well as all other issues of importance would be discussed and voted on.

Discipline is not necessary to deal with disruptive actions: "...when a child of seven makes himself a social nuisance, the whole community expresses its disapproval. Since social approval is something that everyone desires, the child learns to behave well" (Neill 1960, p. 159). Neill was against giving rewards claiming them superfluous and negative. "To offer a prize for doing a deed is tantamount to declaring that the deed is not worth doing for its own sake" (Neill 1960, p. 162). Conversely, Neill felt that punishment also should be avoided. "Punishment is always an act of hate. In the act of punishing, the teacher or parent is hating the child and the child realizes it" (Neill 1960, p. 165).

Dewey felt that the student should be guided, but that education should be self-directed. In terms of handling disruptive behavior I believe that Dewey would have felt the same about teaching subject matter — that the student should be guided but the handling of disruptive behavior and the disruptive behavior of their peers could be self-directed. The only thing required by the student is an interest. "Impulse or interest means to work it out, and working it out involves running up against obstacles, becoming acquainted with materials, exercising ingenuity, patience, persistence, alertness, it of necessity involves discipline — ordering of power — and supplies knowledge. (All the more better that the child is motivated. By necessity they will learn the discipline, since they need it to solve the problem.) For the child to realize his own impulse by recognizing the facts, materials and conditions involved, and then to regulate his impulse through that recognition is education" (Dewey 1902, pp. 39 - 41).

As a way of dealing with classroom disruptions, conflict resolution and mediation programs have been implemented in many schools across the country (Araki, Takeshita and Kadomota 1989; Davis & Porter 1985). These programs are a student-directed effort in which students solve disputes and problems among themselves. These programs allow students to utilize their life experiences and community knowledge in an effort to solve problems.

There has been much recent research in the area of Conflict Resolution and Mediation programs. Mediation programs not only provide alternatives to traditional discipline practices, but also teach students important life skills (Robertson 1991). School-based peer mediation programs operate on the assumption that encouraging students in dispute to work collaboratively, to resolve a present conflict, is a more effective way of preventing future conflict and getting students to learn to take responsibility for their behavior, than punishing students for their actions (Cohen 1987). Additional benefits cited include teaching students nonaggressive conflict resolution skills, improving the overall school climate, and shifting the responsibility for resolving student conflicts to students, enabling teachers to spend more time teaching (Davis and Porter 1985).

There have been several school-based mediation programs across the United States. Although each program has its own unique characteristics, they all basically operate in a similar manner. Usually the entire faculty, staff and student bodies are educated about mediation. School assemblies or classroom instruction is most commonly the forum for this education. Next, selected teachers, administrators and students are trained to be mediators. The length of the training depends on the program. When the mediation program is in operation, students and staff have an option of choosing mediation as a way to settle a dispute. The mediators oversee the resolution of the conflict using the mediation skills they have learned.

With this approach, the responsibility of solving disruptive conflicts is placed in the hands of those having the dispute and other peers who can relate more realistically to the dispute at hand. "Mediation programs already in place illustrate that children and young people are capable — when given the appropriate tools — of handling many of their own conflicts" (Stichter 1986, p. 42). The mediation process serves the purpose of having students deal with their own social problems in a meaningful way that is effective for them individually and effective for the school community.

Class Meetings

I have had a great deal of success having class meetings in my own classroom. We sometimes get so caught up in the academic part of school that we forget that socialization also is important. We need to devote class time to helping students learn how to speak to others and negotiate for what they want. It has been my experience with class meetings that all the members of the class (including myself) learned a great deal about how to talk to each other and problem-solve together. Additionally, we learned how to accept people for who they are. These are skills that serve people well throughout a lifetime. I have observed many general education teachers benefiting from class meetings styled along the "town meeting" model. With larger student groups, the teacher must be more sensitive to assuring participation of all, but many teachers report that the students in their classes are more cohesive, tolerant of one another, and better behaved through the use of class meetings.

A class meeting serves many purposes:

1. It provides an opportunity for the children to express their ideas, anxieties and questions.

2. It gives students time to practice their verbal skills and their growing communications skills.

3. It enables students to interact with each other, to learn to listen, and to respect each other's ideas and comments.

4. It gives the teacher an opportunity to listen to students, to get to know them better and to let them know their views are respected.

5. It is an informal setting, non-threatening to students, open for any topic they would like to discuss.

6. It is an opportunity to invite thoughts and discussions, raise questions, make suggestions, indicate possible directions of activities, introduce provocative ideas and make thought-provoking comments. Some suggestions will work, some will not. The leader can follow the children's response.

7. Meetings provide an atmosphere of community in which everyone can feel accepted.

How to have class meetings:

1. Seat the class in a circle. (A circle is best because anyone who is speaking is visible to everyone else.) Students can be seated on the floor or in chairs.

2. Have students make up meeting rules. I would suggest no more than three rules, i.e., only people with their hand raised will be called upon, one person at a time talks, students not talking will sit and listen without interrupting. By listening and rephrasing, the teacher can mold student suggestions in these three rules. (Decide, as a group, the consequences for people who interrupt.)

3. The meeting leader's job is to make sure the rules are followed, to encourage dialogue, to help students learn to listen to each other and to take turns talking, and to give the students the opportunity to articulate their feelings and ideas. (The leader should know everyone's name.) Unless the purpose of the class meeting is for the leader to get across an idea to the students, the voices of the students will dominate the discussions, not the leader's. The leader may ask the class questions such as, "What do you think of that?" or "Do you agree with Clara?" or "Who would like to add to what Jason has said?" or "Does anyone know why that happens?" It is also the leader's job to limit each student's statement, so no one student is monopolizing the class time. Some groups use a prop, such as a phone receiver, which is passed to the recognized speaker. (The leader can be the teacher, social worker, or even a student under certain circumstances.)

4. It is not unusual to have about 100 class meetings before you hit a good one. Don't get discouraged! Keep in mind that even imperfect meetings can be very positive for the students.

5. The first few class meetings should be short, no longer than 10 or 15 minutes. Discuss the length of meetings with your students to see if they feel they are too long, too short or just right. The younger the students, the shorter the maximum meeting length should be. Try to use the tolerance of the least attentive student as a guideline.

6. Try to listen carefully to your students. You will be a good role model for them in the process of teaching them to listen to each other. Using reflective

listening not only will assure that you truly have understood the speaker, but will model an effective communication tool for your students.

The purpose of reviewing the three learning theories of behaviorism, cognitive processing, and humanism is to gain some understanding of the ways teachers and other educational staff can deal with classroom disruption. Although these theories are distinct from each other, there are some similarities between them. The interest of the students is seen as a key element in both the cognitive and humanist learning perspective.

Additionally, both behavioral theorists and cognitive theorists see modeling as a productive way to teach students. Teachers who are familiar with certain learning theories, and who also feel that their own philosophies are compatible with any given theory, will attempt to define and deal with classroom disruption through that perspective. It would not be unexpected, however, to find a teacher using methods that come from a hybrid theory they have formulated using methods based on practical experience and methodology that comes from a variety of learning theories. I employed techniques from each of the three theoretical perspectives in an attempt to meet the needs of my students. As mentioned at the beginning of this chapter, "espoused theories" and "theories in use" may differ. The beliefs and practices of teachers concerning disruptions in the classroom are directly related to these theories.

The phenomena of classroom disruption like most phenomena can be understood in a variety of ways. The conceptions of those involved often will be different for each individual depending on who they are and the experiences they have had. This is particularly true when comparing the differences in perception between students and teachers. "Many of the taken-for-granteds of adult thinking cannot be taken for granted when it comes to the thinking of children" (Marton 1988, p. 178). The relationship between an individual and aspects of the world around him contribute to that individual's concept of any phenomena. In studying a phenomenon it is essential to describe the relationship between the individuals involved and the phenomena. "Leaving other aspects aside, we end up with categories of description that, though originating from a contextual understanding (interpretation), are decontextualized and, hence, can be used in contexts other than the original one. Above all, they are potential parts of larger structures in which they are related to other categories of description. Such a complex of categories of description is reasonably a very useful tool when it comes to understanding of other people's understanding" (Marton 1988, p. 182).

A conception is a systematic arrangement of ideas; a description of a system that accounts for known or inferred properties. "Concepts reflect and embody in their meaning beliefs about how the world operates, that is, the meaning of concepts is ultimately tied up with the beliefs which their users possess" (Fay 1987, p. 44).

The concept of classroom disruption has several components to it, namely, the definition of disruption, its causes, the consequences of disruption, and how disruption drives the practice of those involved. The relationship between these components also makes up the conception of disruption. Additionally, the differences an individual experiences affects his conception of disruption.

In a study conducted in 1995, a regular education setting and a special education setting were studied for the purposes of understanding how the perception of the components of disruptions drove the practices of the individuals in these settings (Zimmerman 1995). The participants primarily included teachers and the students in the classes. Through observations and interviews, it was determined that disruption meant, on most occasions, that the teacher or a staff member was the party being disrupted. This is an example of a distinction between an espoused theory and a theory in use. The teachers talked about disruption occurring when the learning process of other students was interrupted. In actuality, actions most often were considered disruptive when it was the teacher who was being disrupted.

Disruption occurred usually in the form of students talking, getting out of their seats, or making noises. Serious disruptions were defined as students fighting, yelling loudly and swearing, throwing furniture, and being excessively noncompliant in terms of following a teacher's direction(s). Disruptions caused by events or occurrences other than by students were not considered as much of a concern by the teachers. In all cases, disruption was defined in a behavioristic manner — the disruption was an overt and observable action.

Causes of Disruption: The teachers shared a similar conception of why students were disruptive and, while there was some overlap between the teacher conception and student conception of the causes, there were some differences as well.

Based on the interviews and observations over the year this study was conducted, it was believed that there were two major reasons why the students engaged in disruptive actions. One of these reasons had to do with factors that were unrelated to the school environment and the second reason was indirectly related to the school environment. Generally speaking, the teachers viewed disruption as something that came from within the student that could not be environmentally controlled (Zimmerman 1995).

One reason for the disruptions, they felt, was that the students brought "baggage" with them into the classroom. It was their conception that many of the disruptive students came to the classroom from a dysfunctional home setting. They considered that some students were pre-occupied and upset, due to home-life problems and, consequently, had difficulty following the school's routine and rules. This was, perhaps, the greatest reason for the student's disruptive behavior.

A student's level of frustration, they felt, was another reason that students were disruptive. Frustration was caused by a number of factors, some of which included: a student's inability to understand or complete assignments, a student's need for attention that he may have felt he was not receiving, a student's need to be heard, and a student's inability to follow the rules and routine of the classroom and school. Although, in most cases, the teachers felt that the frustration level of the students was excessively low and, again, assumed that the problem came from within the student. Both teachers in the study stated that when students felt frustrated they often communicated this by acting in a manner that they considered disruptive — such as calling out at whim. Even though the teachers acknowledged that some disruptive actions are forms of communication, — the student's way of getting his point across — they usually treated the disruption as the problem, not as the symptom of the problem.

While some of the students did mention home environment as a cause of disruption, they spoke more about being bored, angry and frustrated when their needs were not being met in the classroom — for instance, not having their questions answered or not being called on in class. Interestingly, it was observed throughout the study that the students were not being disruptive when they were engaged in activity, no matter how dysfunctional their home life was. Also, it was noted that even in the regular education classroom there were students who were not attending to their lessons or to the activity at hand. Subsequently, these students also became disruptive to some degree. Many of the student disrupters had not been described as students with low-frustration levels or as students who came from a dysfunctional home life.

Consequences of Disruption: The consequences of disruption were viewed entirely differently by the students than by the teachers. The consequences in the regular education class were usually seen through the eyes of the students as positive and, most of the time, even enjoyable. A class disruption, if large enough, usually meant a welcome break from whatever task the student was engaged in. Even minimal disruption was viewed as unobtrusive to a student, or if the disruption was directed toward that student (a whispered joke or a passed note), it was viewed as a pleasant experience. At times students would encourage fellow classmates to be disruptive, or they would attempt to prolong the disruption. It was very rare that any student in the regular education class was observed showing displeasure at a disruption, at least until he was caught and punished.

In the special education class, students were much more prone to ignore disruption and carry on with the task at hand. There were, however, times when special education students did seem to enjoy a disruption. Classroom disruption caused anxiety for both teachers, particularly the regular education teacher. It was clearly an unwanted occurrence but when it occurred both teachers took measures to stop it. Additionally, the threat of classroom disruption caused the teachers, particularly the special education teacher, to use preventive measures. And both teachers took steps to have the disruptive students comply with the rules.

Compliance in Regular Education: The basic approach in the regular education setting was a behavioristic approach. This was true for both the perception of what classroom disruption was and how it was handled. Classroom disruption in the regular education class was defined by the teacher. Even though no set behavioristic program, such as behavior modification or behavior contracts, was in place, and the teacher did not identify her use of the behaviorist theory, she did, however, use behavioristic techniques to deal with what she considered to be "classroom disruption." This is, in fact, how she was able to stop the disruptions and have the students comply with the rules. The teacher concentrated on overt behaviors that were observed and she presented stimuli to the students to elicit what she, and other school staff, saw as appropriate actions. Additionally, stimuli were presented to extinguish behavior that was unwanted. Although rewards, such as "star of the week," were introduced to encourage nondisruptive actions and academic achievement, the more common stimuli was to punish disruptive actions. The common forms of punishment were detention, loss of recess, staying after school and phone calls home. There seemed to be a clear understanding, by both staff and students, that actions deemed disruptive by the staff would be punished in some manner, shape or form. The teacher's sole reliance on behavioristic techniques, to deal with classroom disruptions, points to the need to control the classroom environment. Unfortunately this created an atmosphere that was somewhat stifling.

Rogers (1983) claimed that most teachers are, at least in class, impersonal and boring and that many students accept school as an unpleasant experience. Most of what students learn occurs outside of school. The instructor's teaching style of lecture and seat work, presented to students who not only sat in rows but were expected to be in their seat for most of the entire time that they were in the classroom, lent itself to providing an impersonal and sometimes boring environment. Some students in the regular education class felt that their classroom experience was unpleasant. This was particularly true for those students who engaged in classroom disruption. School was irrelevant to them; lessons and seat work were boring and classroom disruption was a tool used to assist in surviving the day. This disruption was most unwelcome by the teacher and, in handling it, the atmosphere of the room would become tense and uncomfortable. The teacher would punish the disrupter either by scolding him in class or by having him do a task that he did not want to do. One form of punishment was to have the disruptive student change his seat. Although, the teacher admitted that this method did not work well to improve the situation no matter how many times the student changed his seat. However, the teacher continued to use the seat-changing strategy which points to the fact that she would rather continue a method that was not working than try something different. Change can be quite uncomfortable and teachers would sometimes prefer an ineffective method than to try something new because they prefer the familiar (Argyris and Schon 1974).

Compliance in the Special Education Classroom: Disruption in the special education classroom also was perceived in behavioristic terms and was handled by utilizing methods that were primarily behavioristic. The stimulus for producing what was perceived by staff as nondisruptive action was most often a reward for what was seen as "good behavior." For disruptive behavior, forms of punishment used were, for example, losing free time or recess time and, on rare occasions, if the disruption was serious and had occurred over a long period of time, the student would lose the chance to participate in a field trip. Rewards came in the form of physical and verbal reinforcements. During an interview the special education teacher repeatedly stated that she used positive reinforcement often and trained her staff to use positive reinforcement as well. Smiles, chatting and teacher proximity serve as reinforcers also (Zimmerman and Zimmerman 1966). These forms of reinforcement, along with affection, were extensively used in the special education class. Tangible reinforcements, however, were not utilized. Additionally, the teacher used social modeling extensively, encouraging her staff to set good examples for the students and encouraging students to be good role models for each other. However, the use of cognitive theory techniques was almost nonexistent in the special education classroom.

As much as the teacher used behavioristic methods, she also extensively used methods that were consistent with the humanistic learning theory. From a humanistic point of view the learning environment should be a place where students feel wanted, cared for and listened to. Rogers talked about a display of real sensitivity and empathic understanding as "when you understand without judging, when you understand what it is like to live in the world of the other person" (Rogers 1987, pp. 40-41). To this end the teacher was a resounding success at creating such a learning environment. The tone of the room during every observation was positive, friendly and surprisingly free of tension. The students seemed happy, energetic, engaged and secure. The students were at ease and comfortable. They asked questions often and, at times, challenged the answers. The response from the teacher and the staff was most often that of acceptance and patience.

Additionally, the teacher talked several times about instilling self-confidence in the students in the class. The first response to disruptive actions, even disruptive actions that were serious, was to talk to the student, not to send them out of the room.

John Dewey stated emphatically that education should be relevant to the student (John Dewey 1902). The teacher's curriculum and instructional style reflected this philosophy. She expended a great deal of energy teaching the class subjects relevant to the students. Fortunately for this teacher she did not have as many curricular constraints as the regular education teacher; she had free reign on what subjects to teach and how to teach them. The teacher reported that she taught subjects that she felt were important for the students to know and that would be valuable to them in their future, but that she also taught subjects she felt the students would find interesting and relevant. The presentation of the material was in varied forms and, whenever possible, the lesson included a hands-on activity. Where the special education class deviated from the humanistic point of view was in its consequences of disruptive actions that could not be handled by just talking with the disrupter. The consequences of classroom disruption, as mentioned earlier, were clearly derived from a behavioristic perspective.

Conception of Disruption Driving Practice: Both teachers struggled to maintain power and control in the classroom. This was more overtly apparent in the regular education class, since in the special education class the struggle for power and control was softened by the teacher's humanistic tendencies. However, since the causes of disruption, as seen through the teachers' eyes, was within the child, the concept driving their practice was to control the students, not necessarily change the environment or instruction style. When the environment was changed it was to accommodate the disruptions within the child.

The methods used to stop disruption were supposed to, somehow, have the students comply with "the law of the land." The law of the land was basically defined by the teacher and the staff, very much in line with behaviorist techniques. There seemed to be a certain amount of anxiety on the part of the teachers, particularly in the regular education setting, about losing control of the class. They saw student compliance as being the key to eliminating the disruptive actions. From this perspective it is easy to understand why both teachers relied heavily on behaviorist methods in order to assure student compliance. However, both the special education and the regular education teachers did have different perspectives, different levels of tolerance for student actions, and different views on whether or not these actions were disruptive or non-disruptive, that drove their own actions in different directions.

Socialization in the Regular Education Class: The regular education teacher viewed socialization in her class as disruptive. She felt that if she allowed the students to socialize she would lose control of them. Therefore she did what she could to prevent socializing — students did not work cooperatively, and were not allowed to talk, students were required to stay in their seats at all times and their desks were arranged in a manner to prevent socialization. She expected students to almost always conform to the classroom rules and norm — the norm being, compliance to the teacher's wishes, sitting quietly and doing assignments.

Also the teacher remained somewhat distant from the students in the class. For example she maintained a formal appearance to keep control of the class. Little social interaction occurred between the teacher and any of the students in class so the students were unfamiliar with her and she, in turn, was unfamiliar with the students in the class. Perhaps this was partially due to the fact that the teacher's perception was that she had too many students to know them all individually, that she did not have enough time, and that the pressure of getting through the curriculum would not allow this type of interaction. It also is possible that she feared losing control of the class through social familiarity. In fact, the teacher seemed determined to keep her students from gaining any power in the classroom because by empowering the students, she would lose control. This belief is consistent with the teacher's sole reliance on behaviorist techniques.

Socialization in the Special Education Class: The teacher was not only tolerant of socialization in the special education class, she encouraged it. She also had a greater tolerance than the regular education teacher for actions that did not always conform to the classroom rules. There seemed to be a wider range of acceptance, on her part, of student action. For example: when an adult was not teaching a lesson to the entire class students were allowed to work cooperatively and a low level of talking was tolerated. The teacher assumed that their work would get done and that a student who was occasionally talking or moving about was not being disruptive.

Even though many of the students in the special education class had histories of frequent volatile actions, the teacher was not observed as having any extreme feelings of anxiety about the possibility of these students becoming extraordinarily disruptive or violent. Although, the teacher and members of the staff were always aware that there were a number of students who could engage in this type of behavior at any time.

The teacher also was much more casual with the students than the regular education teacher was. She shared stories about herself with the students and she joked and laughed with them. She did not hesitate to do these things and she did not appear to have any anxiety that these actions would cause her to lose control of the class. The teacher did not seem to be afraid of the students finding out that she had a sense of humor or finding out that she had some shortcomings as well. In turn, she made a concerted effort to become familiar with her students. She wanted to know how they felt, and often asked them about specific things.

Additionally, she shared power with her students. She tried to give them choices as often as she could, such as giving them the option of sitting where they wanted. By sharing her power she became a more powerful teacher. The students loved her and trusted her, two very powerful feelings.

The Relationship Between the Components of Classroom Disruption: The definition of disruption had a direct effect on the consequences of disruption. As an example, since disruption had been defined, partially, as an interruption in the learning process, particularly interrupting the teacher, the result was a feeling of annoyance or anxiety about the disruption on the part of the teacher. Additionally the definition of disruption affected the driving practice of the participants. Since disruption was defined as something the student did, the practice was driven by the perception that the student needed to change. The perception of the causes of disruption affected the practice of the participants. The students felt that if they were bored they would be more likely to engage in disruptive actions. This was observed during the study — if a student was unengaged or bored in the classroom his response most often was to become disruptive.

The perception by teachers that disruption was caused by a dysfunctional family life also drove their practice. Many of these students received social work services. Additionally, in the regular education class if the perception of the cause had focused more on disruption created by the classroom environment, presumably some of the structure of that class would have been different.

The consequences of disruption clearly drove the practice of all participants. The teacher's anxiety and annoyance, caused by disruption, led her to use methods geared to stopping the disruption. This also was true for the students who acted in a manner to either earn rewards or avoid punishment.

Disruption Observed in the Classroom:

Special Education Class: In the special education class minimal disruption was observed. In fact, most of the observations were uneventful. Since most of the students from this special education class carried a great deal of "baggage," perhaps making them more prone to be disruptive, it may be surprising that there was not more disruption, for this reason alone. Disruption caused by frustration did occur on occasions, particularly when a student wanted some adult attention and did not receive that attention in a timely enough manner for that student. As amazing as this may sound, boredom was not observed in the special education class. During each observation students were engaged in activities, whether it was a full class lesson, a small group lesson, or independent work.

The low amount of disruption was attributed to several factors — the small number of students in the class as well as the large number of adult staff who could attend to these students, the students' needs were attended to almost immediately because of the large staff and, if a student needed some individual attention outside of the class, this also was available without much difficulty. Additionally, the large number of staff increased the ability to monitor disruption when it occurred. It was almost impossible to be disruptive and not "get caught." Students were aware of this fact and were less prone to engage in disruptive actions. In fact, only one incident was observed of a student engaging in a disruptive action that was not seen or heard. The staff provided in-class support for the special education teacher. She had many opportunities to discuss classroom disruption with staff members and, in turn, staff members had many opportunities to talk with her about the same topic.

Another factor that contributed to the minimal amount of classroom disruption in the special education class was the students' frequent opportunities to deal with difficulties they were having. The teacher was usually accessible, both physically and emotionally, to her students and most of the students felt comfortable sharing themselves and their problems with her. Students felt comfortable talking to other staff members as well. The special education program had a built in half-time social worker who worked with the class. Students saw the social worker on a weekly basis and also on an "as-needed" basis. Students viewed the teacher, and most of her staff, as their advocates and people who were on their side.

Students in the special education class were given many opportunities to work cooperatively and socialize with peers and staff. Most students had much to say to each other and to the staff. If given the opportunity to socialize during the day, students were less inclined to engage in talking during lessons and during other activities; their energies were more likely to be spent attending to the lesson or task at hand The students in the special education class were observed talking much less frequently during times when they were supposed to be quiet than the regular education students.

The lively content of the lessons and activities in the special education class also appeared to alleviate much classroom disruption. Students seemed happy and eager to participate in the events of the classroom. Additionally, assignments were individualized so that even if the entire class had the same lesson, the tasks to follow were tailor-made to meet the needs of each student. This reduced the amount of frustration caused by the inability to do the assignment or by the feeling that the assignment was not challenging for the student.

The last, and perhaps, most important factor that contributed to the limited amount of disruption was the pedagogical skills of the staff, particularly of the teacher. She was a warm and friendly person with a good sense of humor. Students felt welcomed in the classroom environment and genuinely liked her, she in turn, genuinely liked them. Generally the interactions between the staff and students were friendly and pleasant. There was always a positive feeling in the room and there was laughter from both the students and the staff.

Regular Education Class: The data observed indicated that slightly more than twice as many disruptive actions occurred in the regular education setting than in the special education setting. Some of this can be explained very simply by the fact that there were 12 more students and only one adult in the regular education class. The students' disruptive actions often were undetected (34 percent), by the regular education teacher. This was partially due to the physical configuration of the room. Students figured out how to "hide" in the rows of desks so that their disruptive actions would be unseen or unheard. With only one staff person and 28 students, it was likely that when the students were being disruptive much of it would not be seen or heard.

Another factor was that students were given almost no legitimate opportunity, during class time, to socialize. Students did socialize, clandestinely, throughout the day. Not surprisingly, more than half of the disruption that took place in the regular education class was in the form of talking.

The nature of the instruction in the room also contributed to disruption. No hands-on activities or any activities that allowed students to get out of their seats were observed. Lessons were delivered in the form of a lecture, followed by a period when the teacher would ask questions about the lecture. After the questions there would be a brief period of time when students did seat work, most often from a textbook or a workbook. Evidence of boredom during every observation was recorded. Some students, who were mildly bored, would jump in and out of attention to lessons. Others would simply not be attentive at all, very often their textbook was not opened to the assigned page. There were many times when students, who were not attending to either a lesson or an assignment, were not being disruptive. There were usually no consequences for this. However, there were times when the teacher would admonish a student if she noticed that they were turned to the wrong page or staring out into space. She would attempt to keep students focused on their lessons by asking questions, especially of those students she knew were not being attentive. But these questions came at the end of a lesson when it was probably too late. During the course of a lecture the teacher reminded students frequently to pay attention. Instruction was not individualized, except for six students who received resource room support. Some students who engaged in disruptive actions may have been frustrated, feeling the work was too challenging or not challenging enough.

Additionally, like most elementary teachers, the teacher had no in-class support. Unlike the special education teacher, who could bounce ideas and thoughts off other staff members, the regular education teacher was the only adult in her classroom. When serious disruptions took place it was handled outside of the class by someone other than she. The usual consequence of a student's serious disruptive action was that he or she would be sent to the office. This, most often, was not viewed positively by the principal and other staff members and was sometimes even seen as a poor reflection on the teacher. Naturally, not wanting to use this option often, the teacher became more concerned and driven to control her students in order to prevent any type of disruption. This, in turn, created a certain anxiety on her part.

Implications: In spite of the fact that there are a variety of ways to view and deal with classroom disruption a behavioristic perspective seemed to be the dominant perspective used in both classrooms. Although behavioristic techniques can be of value, schools and staff may be well advised to explore other options derived from different learning perspectives to deal more effectively with classroom disruption. I would encourage teachers to take some risks in using unconventional methods, particularly when the accepted methods are not working.

Additionally, incorporating the views of the students and including them when creating strategies for dealing with classroom disruption could have countless benefits. At the very least, opening a dialogue between staff and students may provide insights that previously have been ignored.

The results of this study seem to indicate that the more involved students are in their environment, the less likely they are to engage in disruptive actions. This means that classroom instruction and curriculum must be relevant and interesting to the students.

Finally, it seems that one of the most important factors in reducing classroom disruption is to create an environment where all participants feel safe, secure and happy. Providing such will eliminate many of the causes of classroom disruption.

Conclusions: The components of classroom disruption consisted of the "definition" of classroom disruption, the perception of the causes, the consequences and how the perception drove the practice of the participants.

Clearly there was a difference between the participants' conception of classroom disruption in general and a difference in the conception of the components of classroom disruption. Although there were differences between the regular education teacher and the special education teacher, there was a greater difference between the conceptions of both teachers and the conceptions of the students.

Classroom disruption was an important issue to both teachers and both related that it was one of their primary concerns. Both believed that disruptions created an impediment to what generally was felt as their most important goal — creating a successful learning process. Disruption was defined in terms of the actions of the students and meant, on most occasions, that the teacher or a staff member was being disrupted.

The perception of the teachers was that disruption was basically caused by emotional problems related to issues outside of the school environment, such as an upsetting home life, frustration caused by school work that was either too challenging or not challenging enough, and frustration caused by a student's inability to get attention. The perception of the students was that disruption was additionally caused by being bored, being angry, not getting attention fast enough and teachers who, in their opinion, were unfair.

Both teachers felt that it was one of their duties to prevent classroom disruption of all sorts and both generally relied on behaviorist methods to prevent it. However, the special education teacher used many preventative measures to avoid disruption; measures which included aspects of the humanistic theory, i.e., providing students with opportunities to talk about problems, creating an environment in which the students felt safe, secure and happy. The regular education setting used the "star" program, a metacognitive technique in dealing with disruption. This program had almost no impact on students who were chronically disruptive and it had limited success with other students. In addition, a schoolwide mediation program used during the lunch and recess period had almost no affect on classroom disruption.

The results of the behaviorist techniques in the regular education class were successful from the perspective of the teacher. The students, for the most part, were compliant and nondisruptive. Most of the students were compliant in order to avoid punishment; thus, they would engage in disruptive action if they felt that they would not be caught. If a student's disruption became severe or dangerous, the consequence of their disruption was handled outside of the classroom, usually by the building principal. The atmosphere of the regular education program was formal and, at times, tense. There also were times when there was an adversarial relationship between the teacher and the students.

In the special education class, students were nondisruptive for a different reason. They wanted to gain the approval of the teacher and staff. However, the students in this class were almost always engaged in activity because the teacher and staff usually made the content of the activity relevant and interesting to the students. The students' need to be disruptive seemed to be minimal. The atmosphere of the special education class was comfortable, friendly and relaxed. No moments of tension were noted during observations.

Home Interventions

Even in the best of all possible home environments, some individuals will require some behavioral interventions. As an educator, you may see the results of problem behavior at home in the classroom and school. Educators need to help parents understand that before dealing with behavior it is important to recognize when they need to intervene and to ask these three questions:

1. Is the behavior going to cause emotional or physical harm to the individual engaging in the behavior?

2. Is the behavior going to cause emotional or physical harm to others?

3. Can they, as the parent, live with the behavior? If the answer is yes they also might ask themselves for how long. (The banging of a spoon on a table can get to some people after about 32 seconds or less while others may have a greater tolerance for this disruptive behavior.)

I cannot stress enough the fact that when children display inappropriate behavior they need to have consequences for their actions. We do a grave disservice to children when we "excuse" their inappropriate behavior. What we tell them in essence, is that it's okay for them to do whatever they want. Although it is difficult, children with behavior problems can understand right from wrong and can learn to make appropriate choices. If, however, they are excused from all negative behavior then they will never learn how to make better choices in terms of their behavior. All children need to understand how the behavior they exhibit affects others. This is particularly true for children with behavior problems. Research has now shown that children with behavior problems often grow up to be adults with behavior problems.

Educators sometimes will need to assist parents in modifying discipline for children with behavior problems. While it is important to be very structured and to set limits with follow-through, there must be a degree of flexibility involved as well. As with most things, using common sense is always a good idea. Again, if a parent is not sure of what to do in general or in specific situations they should be encouraged to ask people they know and trust and get as much input as possible. Hopefully, one of those people will be an educator.

Even if parents have provided the perfect environment for their child there will be times when it won't be enough. They also need to provide discipline and set limits. Below are intervention strategies that may prove useful. (For more information on the specific strategies see the "School Interventions" section of this chapter.)

Behavior Records

There has been a great deal of success in using behavior modification sheets with children with behavior problems. These sheets help structure a child's life and make clear the specific behaviors the child needs to improve. Educators can assist parents with developing and implementing these sheets. These sheets should be consistent with what is occurring in school in order to create a bridge between school and home.

* * * * * *

© 2000 LRP Publications; all rights reserved.   85

Behavior Modification Chart
Weekly Checkmarks

Name_____

	MON.	TUES.	WED.	THURS.	FRI.
1. Respect other people.					
2. Keep sneakers tied.					
3. Let other people speak.					
4. Complete schoolwork.					
5. Complete chores.					
6. Keep your hands to yourself.					
7. Respect other people's property.					

COMMENTS:

- The child should easily be able to do three of the seven goals on the chart. Four goals should be challenging.

- The child gets a checkmark for each goal he or she achieves during the day.

- The chart should be read with the child. The child should respond with a yes or no to each goal when asked if he or she was able to reach that goal.

- If the child gets all seven checks in a day he or she should receive a small reinforcement (i.e., pencil, sticker, lifesaver, ten minute activity with a parent).

- A weekly reward should also be given. Since it is possible to earn 70 checks, achieving 60 should qualify the child for the weekly reward which could be the following: extra late bedtime, a special outing, a game or toy, special dinner and anything else the child finds motivating. Ask your child what they would like to earn.

- The child should be able to earn extra or bonus checks for exceptional behavior.

* * * * * *

Name_____   Date_____

Behavior Modification Sheet

	Act.1	Act.2	Act.3	Act.4	Act.5	Act.6	Act.7
Follow directions of adults.							
Be a good listener.							
Share with others.							
Show kindness to others.							

- The child should easily be able to do two of the four goals on the chart. Two goals should be challenging.

- The child gets a checkmark for each goal he or she achieves during a period.

- The chart should be read with the child after every activity. The child should respond with a yes or a no to each goal when asked if he or she is able to reach that goal.

- Reinforcement should be given to the child on both a daily and weekly schedule. The child also can be reinforced twice a day, once before lunch and once before he or she goes to bed.

- Eighty percent of goals achieved should qualify the child for the reward. Rewards should be based on identified motivators.

- The child should have an opportunity to earn extra checkmarks for exceptional behavior.

* * * * * *

Using a behavior contract is a great way to get a child involved in taking responsibility for his own behavior. Many of the guidelines for developing contracts of use in the school are also applicable for use in the home. (See below.)

1. Contracts should be written in a collaborative process with the child and the parents and should be written in a positive manner.

2. Expectations should be clear, simple and specific. Parents should explain the exact behavior they are seeking, such as, completing chores, not talking back, etc.

3. Goals should be achievable and specific. (Parents need to understand that behavior does not change over night.)

4. Try to get as many people as possible who are involved with the child to have input in the design of the contract, such as siblings, other relatives who reside in the same home as the child and members of the school staff.

5. Contracts should be tailor-made to each individual child, conducive to each unique home environment.

6. The behavior contract should not be viewed as a punishment, but as an enhancement. This is true for both the child and the parent.

7. All parties concerned should adhere to the terms of the contract. Parents should understand that if they don't follow the terms of the contract their child won't either.

8. Everyone should have a signed copy of the contract, particularly the parent(s) and the child.

See sample on next page.

* * * * *

James
Behavior Contract

Positive Qualities	Areas of Concern
- Positive relationship with parents	- Striking others, especially siblings
- Artistically creative	- Difficulty completing chores
- Can be cooperative and charming	- Inappropriate touching of others
	- Interrupts when others are talking

Goals for Parents to Use to Assist James:

- Controlling his anger by providing alternatives to negative behavior.
- Providing incentives for appropriate behavior.
- Providing alternative space when necessary.

Goals for James to Achieve:

- Special time with a person of his choice.
- Extra privileges.
- Extra recess time.
- Special activities (i.e., cooking).

James is a boy who has many positive attributes. However, at times, he engages in behavior that is both disruptive and inappropriate. James can earn things that he finds enjoyable when he acts appropriately. There will, however, be consequences for negative behavior. When James is engaging in negative behavior the following steps will be taken:

1. James will receive a warning about the inappropriate behavior.

2. If the behavior continues, James will be asked to sit at a designated seat. He will be required to sit in this seat for no less than 10 minutes.

3. If James is unable to maintain himself at the designated seat, he will be required to go to a designated spot out of the immediate area for a period of no less than 30 minutes.

If James exhibits overt aggression toward anyone, he will be removed from the immediate area immediately. He will be required to remain out for at least one hour.

Signatures:_____

_____

★ ★ ★ ★ ★

Oppositional Plans

There may be times when a child becomes unresponsive, uncooperative or totally oppositional at home. Parents need to understand that, in general, it is best to "choose your battles." Children need choices whenever possible. Very often children with behavior problems use inappropriate behavior to avoid situations that are unpleasant to them. When the child becomes oppositional a consistent plan of action is crucial. Educators can assist the parents in designing and implementing an oppositional plan that meets the needs of the child and the parent. See the example below of an oppositional plan that may be useful at home.

Steps for Dealing with Oppositional Behavior

1. When Sue is exhibiting oppositional behavior (not following a reasonable direction) she should be given two prompts (20 seconds between warnings).

2. If after the second prompt the behavior continues, Sue should be told, "You have a choice of following directions or going into the stress-free zone," for at least five minutes. Let Sue decide when she is able to cooperate and follow directions. If she is not ready she should remain in the stress-free zone.

3. If Sue refuses to make a choice, explain that you will make the choice for her and take her to the stress-free zone.

4. Sue should have the option of requesting to go to the stress-free zone and should be encouraged to use this option when she feels herself starting to lose control. Behavior that requires immediate placement in the stress-free zone may include: striking or hurting anyone; throwing furniture; any behavior that is self-injurious or dangerous to others.

A request for Sue to go to the stress-free zone should be presented in a non-punitive manner. Sue should be told that everyone wants to see her happy and safe. Appropriate statements to say could be, "We're sorry you're having such a difficult time." or "It seems you need some time to get yourself together." Or "We want you to feel better." While she is in the stress-free zone supervise her appropriately but do not engage in lengthy conversations. The key is to have some time and a place that has little stimulation but that is safe and comforting.

When using an oppositional plan it is important to help the parent keep in mind that the plan is not a punishment but a tool to be used to help a child when he is unable to make good choices or is out of control. It is important that the child does not feel rejected by the parent.

Chapter Seven

Functional Analysis and Development of Behavior Intervention Plans

Inappropriate behavior is often a manner in which an individual communicates a need. By understanding the function of the communication we can alter the environment or teach substitute methods in order for individuals to get their needs met.

When inappropriate behavior becomes chronic the patterns of the behavior need to be analyzed. Conducting a functional assessment/analysis is an invaluable analytical method. The purpose of functional assessment/analysis is to give equal attention to the function of a behavior as to its form. An analysis of a problem behavior's function in terms of its antecedents and consequences is necessary for the selection of the most effective treatment procedures (Crawford, Brockel, Schauss and Miltenberger 1992).

Inappropriate behavior is often a manner in which an individual communicates a need. By understanding the function of the communication we can alter the environment or teach substitute methods for individuals to get their needs met. Some of the functions of inappropriate behavior may include interactive functions such as requests for attention, social interaction, assistance, or objects (Donnellan, Mirenda, Mesaros and Fassbender 1984). Other functions include negations such as protests, refusals or cessation. Declarations about events, objects, persons, errors or greetings also would be considered functional behavior. Inappropriate behavior can serve other functions such as escape from aversive conditions or internal stimulation. An analysis of the antecedents, behavior and consequences (ABCs) yields information that leads to a hypothesis about why the behavior is occurring and how to deal with it.

Antecedents are the specific setting in which a behavior occurs. To identify the antecedents the following questions must be answered:

- Who is present when the behavior occurs?
- What is going on when the behavior occurs?
- When does the behavior tend to occur?

91

- When does the behavior tend not to occur?

- Where does the behavior tend to occur?

- Where does the behavior tend not to occur?

Specific antecedents could be, but are not limited to: who the individual is sitting next to, hunger, the temperature of the room, or the subject being taught.

Consequences are the actions that usually follow the behavior in that setting. To identify the consequences the following questions must be answered:

- What happens after the behavior occurs?

- What does the staff do?

- What do the other students do?

- What does the individual who engaged in the behavior do?

- What do you think increases the likelihood of the behavior occurring again?

Specific consequences could be, but are not limited to: a teacher's anger, being sent out of the room, other students laughing. Once a functional analysis/assessment is performed a behavior intervention plan suited to the individual can be developed and formulated. The behavior intervention plan should include the following:

Background Information: Include a description of the student such as age, gender and other physical characteristics. Include any relevant information that may explain why inappropriate behavior is occurring, i.e., ADHD, recent death of a loved one, dysfunctional aspects of the family. A description of the classroom, the school programs and school environment also should be included.

Strengths, Areas of Concern and Motivators: Indication of these specific elements is essential in developing an accurate and relevant behavior intervention plan.

Functional Assessment: Define target behavior(s) and describe what observation measures you will use to record the targeted behavior. Explain why you chose specific measures. Identify the antecedents to these behaviors and what you believe is maintaining the behavior (consequences of the behavior).

Intervention Plan: Design an intervention plan for the targeted behavior.

Evaluation: Describe how you will evaluate the effectiveness of the proposed intervention plan. (See below for a sample behavior intervention plan.)

Behavior Intervention Plan

John Doe

John Doe is a fifth-grade student at Washington Elementary School. It is reported that John is displaying distracting, disruptive and oppositional classroom behavior. I had the opportunity to talk with Susan Black, CSE chairperson; Mary Smith, one-to-one aide; Jane Brown, fifth-grade teacher; Laurie Johnson, school social worker; Chris Williams, building principal, and Mr. and Mrs. Doe, John's parents. The educational team, as well as John's parents, was in agreement that John's behavior interferes with his ability to make academic progress.

A physician and a psychologist have identified John as having Attention Deficit Hyperactivity Disorder. Ritalin was prescribed for John. He has been taking Ritalin for approximately two and a half years. John lives with his mother and older sister. John's parents are divorced. His father sees John on a regular basis. Both parents report that John displays similar behavior at home.

The Committee on Special Education classifies John as "other health impaired." He is fully included in a regular fifth-grade class and receives support from a one-to-one aide. School staff describes John as a highly impulsive boy who has a great deal of trouble focusing on his work. Additionally, John becomes easily frustrated which leads to oppositional behavior. It seems that disruptive behavior occurs more frequently during transition times; between activities and during less-structured activities such as lunch and recess. John has few friends. His behavior tends to alienate his fellow classmates.

Observation

I observed John on the morning of April 26. It was apparent that he had a great deal of difficulty remaining focused and sitting still. Behavior displayed by John included rocking in his chair, talking to himself, throwing a pencil, dropping his work sheet, picking his nose, burping and making howling sounds.

John was quite responsive to Mary Smith, his one-to-one aide. However, if John felt that Ms. Smith was not watching, his behavior escalated. John continued to work on assignments throughout my observation, but needed many prompts to stay on task.

Summary of Functional Analysis of Behavior

After observing John and meeting with the educational team, which included the individuals previously mentioned, a Behavior Intervention Plan was developed after a functional analysis of the behavior was conducted.

John's Strengths:

- Bright   - Can be sensitive

- Responsive to adults   - Can be charming

- Has shown improvement   - Enjoys helping others

*Possible Motivators:

- Earning the privilege of spending "special time" with a staff person of John's choice

- Earning free time where John can pick any activity he wants

- Earning the use of a Walkman

- Earning stickers, pencils, food or other tangible objects

- Earning extra time on the computer

- Earning "special" privileges

*Ask John for additional motivators

Behavior:

- Calls out frequently   - Verbally aggressive at times

- Makes noises   - Physically aggressive at times

- Out of seat   - Does not complete school work
                                        or homework

Antecedents (When behavior is likely to occur)	*Consequences (Maintains the behavior)*
- Long work periods that require sitting	- John gets out of doing tasks
- Repetitious work assignments	- John gets to move
- Challenging work assignments	- Peers laugh
- Less structured activities	- Staff members become angry
- supervised activities	- Attention from others

Hypothesis:

When John is engaged in challenging and repetitious assignments he loses his focus quickly. He begins to call out and/or make body noises and, at times, escalates to verbal and physical aggression. This behavior often is reinforced because John avoids doing what he does not want to do.

It is important for those working with John to realize that he will exhibit inappropriate and disruptive behavior that is sometimes out of his control. The keys to successful improvement in this area are to provide gentle but firm guidelines for John and to help provide strategies for John to use when he has difficulty controlling his own actions. It is important that the staff people working with John operate as a team to implement this Behavior Intervention Plan. This will assist in providing a consistent program, something that is essential for John.

Evaluation:

Team members should meet every two weeks (more if necessary) to review the Behavior Intervention Plan and make modifications as necessary.

Suggestions

Environmental Strategies:

- Continued provision of a *structured* and *consistent* environment. It should be very clear to John what the expectations and rules are. Post rules conspicuously where they are visible to John.

- Continue to support and encourage John as much as possible. Positive reinforcement for appropriate behavior is essential. Identify exactly what you are reinforcing — "I like it when. . ." not "You're a good boy."

- Consistent and swift response to inappropriate behavior. John needs to see consequences for behavior as quickly as possible. He should be prompted when he needs to be re-directed. Consequences should be addressed in a non-judgmental way, never dredging up old times, either positive or negative.

- Staff should refrain from excessively cajoling John to do things. Clear limits should be set for John and follow-through of consequences is vital.

- Administration of consequences should be done in a calm manner. Getting angry, yelling or humiliating John will have a negative impact on the situation.

- Include John in behavioral planning so that he feels he has some control in the situation and that he may become invested in any plans.

- Encourage extracurricular activities so that John can benefit from positive peer models.

- "Choose your battles." Try and ignore as much inappropriate behavior as possible.

- John should be given choices for behavior as often as possible. Choices should be realistic not "devil or the deep blue sea."

- It may be useful to conduct weekly class meetings. This will help John attain more positive interaction skills and provide an opportunity for the rest of the class to talk about issues and concerns. (Class meeting information sheet included in report.)

- Use of non-verbal cues with John may be beneficial. (Tactile — hand on shoulder. Visual — gestures.)

- When verbal cues are needed go over to John and tell him directly. Don't give him directions or re-direct him from across the room.

- Pre-set John before new activities. Go over academic and behavioral expectations before the activity begins.

- Keep directions short and simple. If you give John a multi-step direction, give it in parts. Use multi-part directions to allow legitimate "walking around time."

Specific Interventions:

- Use of a behavior modification plan. (An example is included in this report.)

- Use of an Oppositional Plan when John is exhibiting inappropriate, oppositional or disruptive behavior.

- Provision of a "stress-free zone" in the classroom. When John requires this space, either at his own request or at the request of a teacher, John should be left alone (shadowed by his educational assistant) until he is ready to join the group.

- Provide John with an older peer buddy to model positive social interactions.

- Provide opportunities for John to work with younger or less capable students. This may increase his self-esteem and create positive feelings about him. Giving John other responsibilities also will be helpful.

- Teach John to visualize stressful situations and solutions to problems before he is actively engaged in those situations. (Walking in the hall, recess, etc.) (See information sheet included.)

- Provide appropriate strategies for John to use when he is upset. (Talk to someone, request time alone, ask to take a walk, etc.)

- Teach peers to provide appropriate feedback to John.

- Weekly counseling sessions by the school social worker or psychologist. Sessions should provide an opportunity for play therapy and for John to talk about problems and feelings.

Academic Modifications:

Along with other academic modifications that are already in place the following also may be helpful:

- Provide plenty of hands-on activities.

- Alternate sedentary tasks with more lively activities.

- Activities should be scheduled for no longer than 20-30 minutes.

- After sitting for more than 20 minutes John should be given the option of going for some sort of brief walk.

- For variety, John should occasionally do assignments on a computer.

- Provide a set of materials in each class. Materials should include a writing implement, paper and any books John may need. These materials should not leave the room.

- A multisensory approach to assignments would assist John. Fulfilling some of his assignments in an oral manner would help motivate John to do tasks such as homework.

- Copying notes from the board may, at times, be difficult for John. If possible have notes copied for him or Xeroxed from texts. John could use a highlight marker.

- Remove pages from workbooks or reading material and present them to John one at a time, rather than allowing him to become anxious with workbooks or texts.

- Allow John to tape-record lectures. The tape recorder should be left on top of his desk. If this becomes problematic, the tape recorder could be left on the teacher's desk.

* * * * * *

John Doe

Date_____

Behavior Modification Sheet

	Act.1	Act.2	Act.3	Act.4	Act.5	Act.6	Act.7
Put things back where they belong.							
Keep hands to self.							
Follow directions of teacher and staff.							
Keep desk clean.							
Complete tasks.							

- John should easily be able to do two of the five goals on the chart.

- John gets a check mark for each goal he achieves during an activity.

- The chart should be read *with* John after every activity. He should respond with a yes or no to each goal when asked if he was able to reach that goal.

- This should be done as soon as possible after each activity. This also may help John transition to the next activity more easily.

- A daily and weekly reward can be given.

- Reinforcing rewards for John could be the following: spending "special time" with a staff person of his choice, extra free time, computer time or tangible rewards such as markers, crayons and food. In order to receive the reward John should earn 80 percent of all possible check marks.

- Provide opportunities for John to earn extra check marks.

Roles for Specific Members of the Behavior Management Team

Principal:

- Provide support for teachers and staff to ensure consistent follow-through on agreed-upon behavior management plan.

- Provide a Respite Room that is safe and non-stimulating.

- Provide reinforcement for positive behavior as specified by the teachers.

- Provide parent contact when necessary.

- Coordinate team staff meetings.

Social Worker:

- Provide support for teachers and staff to ensure consistent follow- through on agreed-upon behavior management plan.

- Oversee coordination of Respite Room.

- Provide weekly counseling sessions for John.

- Conduct class meetings.

- Parent contact when necessary.

Psychologist:

- Provide support for teachers and staff to ensure consistent follow- through on agreed-upon behavior management plan.

- Advocate for John's academic and behavioral needs.

- Monitor behavior/John's progress.

- Provide technical assistance when necessary to modify the behavior management plan.

One-to-one Aide:

- Monitor the behavior modification plan.

- Monitor the Respite Plan.

- Maintain close supervision of John.

- Monitor hall behavior and behavior in special area classes.

- Report both positive and negative behavior.

- Assist John in maintaining appropriate behavior.

- Maintain with consistency the terms of the behavior program.

Teacher:

- Modify curriculum as necessary.

- Supervise and communicate with the one-to-one aide, providing assistance when necessary.

- Oversee and modify the behavior management plan as necessary.

- Parent contact when necessary. (A daily notebook may be useful for at least two months after the behavior management plan has been introduced.)

Parents:

- Maintain close communication with key members of the team

- Inform members of the team of any unusual occurrences at home, (loss of a grandparent, getting a new pet, etc.).

- Reinforce the behavior management plan at home.

- Support the team effort at school.

- Encourage John to be successful in school.

John:

- Inform staff people when he is having difficulty.

- Inform staff members if John feels modifications are necessary.

References

Adair, J. G., and Schneider, J. L. (1993). Banking on learning. *Teaching Exceptional Children* 25 (2): 30-34.

Angulo, L. (1988). An exploration of teachers' mental processes. *Teaching and Teacher Education* 4 (3): 231-46.

Araki, C. T.; Takeshita, C.; and Kadomoto, L. (1989). *Research results and final report for the dispute management in the school's project.* (Report No. EA 021399). Manoa: University of Hawaii, Program on Conflict Resolution. (ERIC Document Reproduction Service No. ED 312 750).

Argyris, C., and Schon D. A. (1974). *Theory in education: Increasing professional effectiveness.* San Francisco, CA: Jossey-Bass, Inc.

Bandura, A. (1965) Behavior modification through modeling procedures. In *Research in behavior modification,* ed. L. P. Krasner and L. Ullman. New York: Holt, Rinehart and Winston.

Bandura, A. (1969). *Principles of behavior modification.* New York: Holt, Rinehart and Winston.

Bandura, A. (1971). *Social learning theory.* Morristown, NJ: General Learning.

Bates, P. E. (1982). *Behavior management.* Technical Assistance Services: Illinois special needs populations. (Report No. CE 035 304). Illinois State University. (ERIC Document Reproduction Service No. ED 227277).

Birnbrauer, J. S.; Burchard, J. D.; and Burchard, S. N. (1970). Wanted: Behavior Analysts. In *Behavior modification: The human effort,* ed. R. H. Bradfield. San Raphael, CA: Dimensions Publishing Co.

Bruner, J. (1966). *Toward a theory of instruction.* Cambridge, MA: Harvard University Press.

Bruner, J. (1969). *The process of education.* Cambridge, MA: Harvard University Press.

Cameron, M. I., and Robinson, V. M. (1980). Effects of cognitive training on academic and on-task behavior of hyperactive children. *Journal of Abnormal Child Psychology* 8 (3): 405-19.

Clark, C. M., and Yinger, R. J. (1978). *Research on Teacher Thinking.* (Report No. SP 013 3150). Michigan State University. (ERIC Document Reproduction Service No. ED 160 592).

Clarke, D. D.; Parry-Jones, W.; Gay, B. M.; and Smith, C. (1981). Disruptive incidents in secondary school classrooms: a sequence analysis approach. *Oxford Review of Education* 7 (2): 111-32.

Cohen, R. (1987). School-based mediation programs: Obstacles to implementation. *NAME News* 10: 1-4.

Crawford, J.; Brockel. B.; Schauss, S.; and Miltenberger, R. (1992). A comparison of methods for the functional assessment of stereotypical behavior. *The Journal of the Association for Persons with Severe Handicaps* 17: 77-86.

Davis, A. (1986). Teaching Ideas: Dispute resolution at an early age. *Negotiation Journal* 287-97.

Davis, A., and Porter, K. (1985). Tales of schoolyard mediation. *Update on Law-Related Education* 9 (1): 21-28.

Day, J.D.; French, L.A.; and Hall L.K. (1985). Social influences on cognition development. In *Metacognition, cognition, and human performance*, ed. D. L. Forrest-Pressley, G. E. Mackinnon, and T. G. Waller, 33-56. Orlando, Florida: Academic Press, Inc.

Derry, S. J., and Murphy, D. A. (1986). Designing systems that train learning ability: From theory to practice. *Review of Educational Research* 56:1-39.

Dewey, J. (1900). *The school and society.* Chicago: University of Chicago Press.

Dewey, J. (1902). *The child and the curriculum.* Chicago: University of Chicago Press.

Donnellan, A.; Mirenda, P.; Mesaros R.; and Fassbender, L. (1984). Analyzing the communicative functions of aberrant behavior. *The Journal of the Association for Persons with Severe Handicaps* 9: 201-12.

Douglas, D. I.; Parry, P.; Marton, M.; and Garson, C. (1976). Assessment of a cognitive training program for hyperactive children. *Journal of Abnormal Child Psychology* 4 (4): 389-409.

Fay, B. (1987). *Critical Social Science.* Ithaca, NY: Cornell University Press

Feldman, C. (1994. October 7). Inclusion of disabled. *The Schenectady Gazette*, p. A2.

Fish, M. C., and Mendola, L. R. (1986) The effect of self-instruction training on homework completion in an elementary special education class. *School Psychology Review* 15 (2): 268-76.

Foster-Johnson, L., and Dunlap, G. (1993). Using functional assessment to develop effective, individualized interventions for challenging behaviors. *Teaching Exceptional Children* (Spring): 44-50.

Gagne, R. M. (1985). A theory of instruction. In *Instructional Technology: Foundations*, ed. R. M. Gagne, 49-83. Hillsdale, NJ: Lawrence Erlbaum Associates.

Gagne, R. M., and Glaser, R. (1987). Foundations in learning research. In *Instructional Technology: Foundations*, ed. R. M. Gagne, 49-83. Hillsdale, NJ: Lawrence Erlbaum Associates.

Hackney, H. (1974). Applying behavior contracts to chronic problems. *School Counselor* 22 (1): 23-30.

Heckman, M., and Rike, C. (1994). Westwood early learning center. *Teaching Exceptional Children* (Winter): 30-35.

Huhn, R. H. (1981). *RSM2P: A meta-cognitive approach for teaching cognitive strategies to facilitate learning*. Lake Charles, LA: McNeese State University. (ERIC Document Reproduction Service No. ED 211946).

James, D. H. (1990). *Behavior Modification: Reducing and controlling calling out behaviors*. (ERIC Document Reproduction Service No. ED 319171).

Joyce, B., and Weil, M. (1986). *Models of teaching*. Englewood Cliffs, NJ: Prentice-Hall, Inc.

Keirsey, D. W. (1969). Systematic exclusion: Eliminating chronic classroom disruptions. In *Behavioral counseling: Cases and techniques*, ed. J. Krumboltz and C. Thorensen. New York: Holt, Rhinehart and Winston.

Larson, K. A., and Gerber, M. M. (1984). *Social meta-cognition: The efficacy of cognitive training for social adjustment of learning disabled delinquents*. Santa Barbara, CA: California University. (ERIC Document Reproduction Service No. ED 253 034).

Mace, C. F.; Page, T. J.; Ivancic, M. T.; and O'Brien, S. (1986). Effectiveness of brief time-out with and without contingent delay: A comparative analysis. *Journal of Applied Behavior Analysis* 19: 79-86.

Marton, F. (1988). Phenomenography: Exploring different conceptions of reality. In *Qualitative Approaches to Evaluation in Education*, ed. D. Fetterman, 176-205. Wesport, CT: Greenwood Publishers.

Meichenbaum, D., and Asarnow, J. (1979). Cognitive-behavioral modification and metacognitive development: Implications for the classroom. In *Cog-

nitive-Behavioral Interventions: Theory, Research and Procedures, ed. P. C. Kendall and S. D. Hollon, 11-35. New York: Academic Press.

Meichenbaum, D., and Goodman, J. (1971). Training impulsive children to talk to themselves: A means of developing self-control. *Journal of Abnormal Psychology* 2: 115-26.

Neill, A. S. (1960). *Summerhill*. New York, NY: Hart Publishing Company.

Nespor J., and Barylske J. (1991). Narrative discourse and teacher knowledge. *American Educational Research Journal* 28 (4): 805-23.

Nisbett, R. E.; Fong, G. T.; Lehman, D. R.; and Cheng, P. W. (1987). Teaching Reasoning. *Science* 238: 625-31.

Parsavand, S. (1994. December 18). Inclusion changing education. *The Schenectady Gazette*, p. A1.

Patterson, G. R., and Bank, L. (1986). Bootstrapping your way in the nomological thicket. *Behavioral Assessment* 8: 49-73.

Poteet, J. A. (1973). *Behavior Modification*. Minneapolis, MN: Burgess Publishing Company.

Reinert, H. R., and Huang, A. (1987). *Children in conflict*. Columbus, OH: Merrill.

Robertson, G. (1991). *School-Based Peer Mediation Programs: A natural extension of developmental guidance programs*. (Report No. CG 024334) (ERIC Document Reproduction Service No. ED 346 425).

Rogers, C. (1983). *Freedom to Learn: For the 80s*. Columbus, OH: Merrill.

Rogers, C. (1987). The underlying theory: Drawn from experience with individuals and groups. *Counseling and Values*. Columbus, OH: Merrill.

Shier, T. (1969). Applying systematic exclusion to a case of bizarre behavior. In *Behavioral counseling: Cases and techniques*, ed. J. Krumboltz and C. Thorensen. New York: Holt, Rhinehart and Winston.

Shuell, T.J. (1990). Phases of meaningful learning. *Review of Education Research* 60: 531-47.

Skinner, B. F. (1954). The science of learning and the art of teaching. *Harvard Educational Review* 24: 86-97.

Skinner, B. F. (1971). *Beyond freedom and dignity*. New York: Knopf.

Smith, M., and Misra, A. (1992). A comprehensive management system for students in regular classrooms. *The Elementary School Journal* 92 (3): 353-72.

Stichter, C. (1986). When tempers flare, let trained student mediators put out the flames. *American School Board Journal* 173 (3): 41-42.

Sulzer-Azaroff, B., and Mayer, G. R. (1977). *Applying behavior-analysis procedures with children and youth.* New York: Holt, Rinehart and Winston.

Taber, J., Glaser, R., and Halmuth, H. (1967). *Learning and programmed instruction.* Reading, Massachusetts: Addison-Wesley Publishing Company, Inc.

Thomas, G. P. and Ezell, B. (1972). The contract as a counseling technique. *Personnel and Guidance Journal* 51 (1): 27-31.

Waksman, M. (1985). *Developing metacognitive awareness: An alternative instructional model.* Toronto, Ontario: Center for Cognitive Education. (ERIC Document Reproduction Service No. ED 269 170).

Walker, H., and Sylwester, R. (1991). Where is school along the path to prison? *Educational Leadership* (September): 14-16.

Weinstein, C. E., and Mayer, R. E. (1986). The reaching of learning strategies. In *Handbook of research on teaching,* ed. M. C. Wittrock, 315-327. New York: Macmillan.

Yau, C. (1991). An essential interrelationship: Healthy self-esteem and productive creativity. *Journal of Creative Behavior* 25 (2): 154-61.

Zimmerman, B. F. (1995). *The nature and consequences of classroom disruption.* Ann Arbor, MI: UMI Dissertation Services.

Zimmerman, B. F. (1998). Classroom disruption: Educational theory as applied to perception and action in regular and special education. In *Advances in special education,* ed. A. Rotatori, J. Schwenn and S. Burkhardt, 77-98. Greenwich, CT: JAI Press Inc.

Zimmerman, E. H., and Zimmerman, J. (1966). The alteration of behavior in a special classroom situation. In *In control of human behavior,* ed. R. Ulrick and T. Stachnick, 94-96. Glenville, IL: Scott, Foresman.